FIRSTS, LASTS
& ONLYS
CRICKET

FIRSTS, LASTS
& ONLYS

PAUL DONNELLEY

PRESENTS THE MOST AMAZING

CRICKET

FACTS FROM THE LAST 500 YEARS

HAMLYN

DEDICATION

Dedicated, with all m[...] love, to my wonderful wife [...] beautiful [...]e,
Karima, who makes [...]rything in my life [...] [...]ly [...] [...]o
enjoyable – *Je t'aime* [...] [...] [...]n
smaller token of everyt[...]

An Hachette UK Company
www.hachette.co.uk

First published in Great Britain in 2010 by
Hamlyn, a division of Octopus Publishing Group Ltd
Endeavour House
189 Shaftesbury Avenue
London
WC2H 8JY
www.octopusbooks.co.uk

ISBN 978-0-600-62173-7

A CIP catalogue record for this book is available from the
British Library

Printed and bound in China

10 9 8 7 6 5 4 3 2 1

THE FIRSTS

THE FIRST

THE FIRST (cont.)

THE FIRST (cont.)

THE FIRST (cont.)

THE FIRST (cont.)

THE FIRST (cont.)

THE FIRST (cont.)

THE FIRST (cont.)

THE LASTS

THE LAST

THE LAST (cont.)

THE LAST (cont.)

THE ONLYS

THE ONLY

THE ONLY (cont.)

THE ONLY (cont.)

THE ONLY (cont.)

THE ONLY (cont.)

THE ONLY (cont.)

INTRODUCTION

Cricket is a sport played all over the world – one has only to consult that yellow-jacketed bible of the sport *Wisden Cricketers' Almanack* each April to read international accounts of the sport – but it is most popular in those parts of the world where the English have had the most influence, which probably explains why it has never really taken off in Scotland or the United States of America.

This book contains a multitude of cricket stories – from the first reference to the sport (in France!) through 'timeless' Tests and One Day Internationals to the latest innovations, such as umpires watching on television, neutral umpires and Twenty20 matches.

This small book is not intended to be a comprehensive history of cricket but it will hopefully find favour with cricket fans, young and old, as they dip into tales of cricketers past and present. The book can be read in one sitting, dipped into at will or even used as a quiz book during the lunch or tea intervals, or those interminable times in English summers when bad light or rain stop play.

If you intend to use it as a quiz book, then these posers might get you started...

* *When was the first County Championship match rained off?*
* *Who is the only player to twice break the world record for the highest individual score in First Class cricket?*
* *Why do pink balls fare better than white ones?*
* *Who was the first professional cricketer to captain England? (The year before he was also the first Test batsman given out for obstructing the field!)*
* *Which two countries took part in the first international outside the British Isles?*
* *In which county were cricketers first fined for playing on the Sabbath?*
* *Who were the first brothers to open the batting for England?*
* *What was responsible for the last two Test matches to be abandoned without a ball being bowled?*

This book could not have been written without the inspiration that was Jeremy Beadle, MBE. He was a most brilliant oddity hunter – the broadcaster Michael Aspel labelled him 'the nation's curator of oddities' – a generous mentor and a warm-hearted friend to many, many people.

I would also like to thank the following for help, inspiration and kindness: Rodney Dale, Trevor Davies at Hamlyn, my agent Chelsey Fox, Ian Harrison, Albert Jack, Mitchell Symons and Jane Birch.

P.D. Donnelley
Oran, Algeria and Essex, England, 2010
www.pauldonnelley.com

ABBREVIATIONS

BCCI – Board of Control for Cricket in India
CCC – County Cricket Club
ECB – England and Wales Cricket Board
ICC – International Cricket Council (formerly Imperial Cricket Conference and International Cricket Conference)
JPL – John Player League
MCC – Marylebone Cricket Club
ODI – One Day International
PCA – Professional Cricketers' Association
SAB – South African Breweries
TCCB – Test and County Cricket Board
WSC – World Series Cricket

NICKNAMES

Aussies – Australia
Kiwis – New Zealand
Springboks – South Africa (Name used in preference to Proteas because it is more recognizable)
Windies – West Indies

NOTE

All matches featured in this book after 1864 are assumed to be First Class unless specifically stated otherwise.

Where known, events are recorded here on the day they happened. For example, Lala Amarnath was the first Indian batsman to score a Test century at home. Although the match began on 15 December 1933, he did not hit his ton until the third day, 17 December, and so the story is recorded under this date (see page 169). Where a match lasted more than one day, the date given – unless it refers to a specific event – is the first day of the match.

Records are accurate up to 10 March 2010.

THE FIRST
CERTAIN REFERENCE
TO CRICKET
FRANCE. DECEMBER 1478.

The first probable reference to the game was in the Wardrobe accounts of Edward I, published by the London Society of Antiquaries. Translated from the Latin, it reads:

'To Master John of Leek, Chaplain of Prince Edward, the King's son, for ready money disbursed by the said prince's playing at Creag' and other sports, out of his and deputies' hands [was paid] at Westminster, on the 10th day of March [1300] the sum of 100 shillings [worth about £2,500 today]. And to his Chamberlain Hugo, at Newenton, in the month of March 20 shillings [£500]. In all £6 [£3000].'

The apostrophe after Creag is a shorthand method for 'et'. Creaget was probably pronounced 'craiget'. We can be almost certain that Creaget was cricket – no one has come up with a plausible alternative. Edward, the first Prince of Wales and later King Edward II, was 16 in 1300. The first certain reference to cricket occurred in December 1478. A document mentions 'criquet' near St Omer, north eastern France.

THE FIRST
RECORDED GAME IN
ENGLAND
Guildford, Surrey, England. 1550s.

On 16 January 1598, 59-year-old coroner John Derrick was involved in a legal dispute over an area of land in Guildford, Surrey. Derrick stated that 'when I was a scholler in the free school of Guldeford, I and several of my fellowes did runne and play there krickett and other plaises'. Therefore, it can be ascertained that cricket was played there in the 1550s during the reign of Queen Mary I.

THE FIRST
CRICKETERS FINED FOR PLAYING ON THE SABBATH

SIDLESHAM, SUSSEX, ENGLAND, EASTER SUNDAY 24 MARCH 1611.

Two men, Richard Latter and Bartholomew Wyatt, were prosecuted in Sidlesham, south of Chichester in West Sussex, for playing cricket instead of going to church on Easter Sunday. They were arraigned by the churchwarden and then tried in Chichester Cathedral, found guilty and each fined a shilling (about £4.90). The church in and around Chichester obviously took a dim view of Sabbath cricketers. In 1622, six men were fined for playing cricket on the Sabbath in a churchyard in Boxgrove, north of Chichester.

THE FIRST
RECORDED MATCH

COXHEATH, KENT, ENGLAND. FRIDAY 29 MAY 1646.

The first recorded game of cricket was played on Coxheath, common land near Maidstone in Kent. It was the first contest in which all the participants were named and was a match between Thomas Harlackenden and Samuel Filmer against Walter Francklyn, Richard Marsh, William Cooper and Robert Saunders, all from Maidstone. It was also the first match on which a bet was placed. William Wood bet Nicholas Hunt a dozen candles that Harlackenden and Filmer would lose. The two beat the four but Wood reneged on his bet.

THIS MATCH ALSO HAD: The FIRST recorded bet on a match

THE FIRST

RECORDED GAME OUTSIDE
THE BRITISH ISLES

ALEPPO, SYRIA. TUESDAY 6 MAY 1676.

The first recorded game outside the British Isles took place at the Green Plat, a valley 4 miles (6.4 km) outside Aleppo (in modern-day Syria). Forty crew members of a ship that had docked at the city, plus the local consul, pitched a tent and indulged in several sports and games including 'duck-hunting, fishing, shooting, hand-ball, krickett...'

THE FIRST
ADVERTISEMENT FOR A
CRICKET MATCH

***The Post Boy*, London, England. Saturday 30 March 1700.**

The first advertisement publicizing a cricket match was published in *The Post Boy*. It told 'gentlemen, or others, who delight in cricket playing, that a match of cricket, of ten gentlemen on each side will be played on Clapham Common... on Easter Monday'.

THE FIRST
RECORDED
GAME BETWEEN
TWO COUNTIES

Kent v Surrey at Dartford Brent, Kent, England.
Wednesday 29 June 1709.

The first recorded game took place between Kent and Surrey at Dartford Brent, Kent although no scorecard exists as to the complete result.

THE FIRST

RECORDED INCIDENCE
OF RAIN STOPPING PLAY

LONDON V ROCHESTER PUNCH CLUB SOCIETY AT WHITE CONDUIT FIELDS, ISLINGTON, LONDON, ENGLAND. MONDAY 1 SEPTEMBER 1718.

The first recorded incidence of 'rain stopped play' occurred at White Conduit Fields, Islington, north London in a match between London and the Rochester Punch Club Society. The match was also the first record of a cricket match involving a club side. The team from Rochester complained that 'the rains, which fell so heavy, [made] it... impossible to continue the game'. That was not the end of the matter and the team was taken to court at Guildhall where the Lord Chief Justice insisted that the game was completed in the following season. The winners received £60 (about £5,000 in today's terms) but by the time the legal costs were taken into account the sum involved in the dispute was nearly £200 (almost £17,000 today).

THIS MATCH WAS ALSO: The FIRST record of a match involving a club side

THE FIRST

REFERENCE TO A BOUNDARY

LONDON V SEVENOAKS AT KENNINGTON COMMON, SURREY, ENGLAND. MONDAY 12 JULY 1731.

The first reference to a boundary was in 1731 when a rope was placed on the edge of the field of play on Kennington Common. However, the boundary rope was not to mark the place to score fours or sixes – all runs were run in those days – it was to keep spectators off the pitch. The first boundary as we know it today was at Tank Malling in Kent in 1841. Until 1910 to score a six a player had to hit a ball out of the ground, not just over the boundary.

THE FIRST

PUB NAME TO COMMEMORATE CRICKET

THE ELEVEN CRICKETERS, WROTHAM ROAD, MEOPHAM, GRAVESEND, KENT, ENGLAND. 1735.

It was in 1735 that the first pub changed its name to commemorate cricket. The pub opened as The Mitre and Sceptre before changing its name to The Leather Bottle. In 1712 it became The Swan (sometimes called The Old Swan), changing again in 1728 to become The Harrow. Seven years later, it became The Eleven Cricketers, a name that stood until 1783. It is now a private house called Basque Cottage. The pub was run by the sister of Valentine Romney, then regarded as 'the best cricket-player in the world'.

THE FIRST

REFERENCE TO AN INJURY CAUSED BY A BOUNCER

KENNINGTON COMMON, SURREY, ENGLAND. JUNE 1736.

Batsmen being injured by bouncers is not a new phenomenon. The earliest record we have of a player being hurt by a bouncer dates back almost 300 years. The batsman's name is lost to posterity but at a game on Kennington Common, he tried to defend himself from a chest-high ball only for it to be deflected off the bat and into his face, breaking his nose. A year later, on the same ground, another batsman was knocked unconscious by a delivery.

THE FIRST

KNOWN PICTURE OF CRICKET

Francis Hayman, *Cricket on the Artillery Ground, Finsbury*. 1743.

The earliest known picture of a game of cricket is entitled *Cricket on the Artillery Ground, Finsbury* and was painted by Francis Hayman in 1743. The painting shows two batsmen and a bowler wearing white shirts, breeches, white knee-length stockings and shoes with buckles. A wicketkeeper has the same outfit but wears a waistcoat in addition, while an umpire and scorer wear three-quarter-length coats and tricorn hats.

THE FIRST

WRITTEN LAWS

London, England. 1744.

Two 'Laws' from the 17th century stated that a batsman could be out caught, and if there was a chance of a batsman being caught he was within his rights to charge the fielder in an attempt to make him fumble the catch.

The first written Laws of the game were produced in 1744, following a meeting of the London Star and Garter Club. One of the Laws laid down that the pitch should be 22 yards (20 m) in length. Previously, the 1727 Articles of Agreement, a basic agreement between the Duke of Richmond and Mr Broderick, had stipulated a pitch 23 yards (21 m) long. On 18 June 1744 the All-England club played Kent at the Artillery Ground, near Finsbury Park, London, under the new rules. This is the first major match for which the full scorecard has survived, although the card for an earlier unimportant contest is extant. The Star and Garter Club revised the Laws in 1755. In 1782 some members of the club formed the White Conduit Club, which merged with the nascent Marylebone Cricket Club five years later.

THIS MATCH WAS ALSO: The FIRST major match for which the full scorecard survives

THE ONLY
HEIR TO A THRONE KILLED
BY A CRICKET BALL

FREDERICK LOUIS, PRINCE OF WALES, LEICESTER HOUSE, LEICESTER SQUARE, LONDON, ENGLAND. WEDNESDAY 20 MARCH 1751.

The unloved and unlovely Frederick Louis, Prince of Wales died aged 44 leaving his younger brother George – later Mad King George III – heir to the throne. Frederick disliked and was disliked by his own father George II whom he continually pestered for money. The prince was a keen cricketer captaining sides for Surrey and London. An abscess in his lung burst by a blow from a cricket ball is said to have brought about his death. A rhyme of the time summed up the public feeling:

Here lies poor Fred who was alive and is dead,
Had it been his father I had much rather,
Had it been his sister nobody would have missed her,
Had it been his brother, still better than another,
Had it been the whole generation, so much better for the nation,
But since it is Fred who was alive and is dead,
There is no more to be said!

THE FIRST
RECORDED
MATCH ON ICE

HEXHAM, NORTHUMBERLAND, ENGLAND. SATURDAY 18 JANUARY 1766.

A frozen River Tyne at Hexham was host to the first recorded mention of cricket being played on ice in January in 1766. More than one hundred years later on 22 January 1879 a thousand people gathered on a frozen dam near Brampton to watch Chesterfield play Sheffield in a game of cricket on ice. The game was played under the usual rules except a player had to retire when he had scored 25 runs. Chesterfield scored 113 in their knock with Test cricketer Harry Charlwood and C.H. Trown scoring the maximum 25 and Joe Rowbotham taking four wickets. Sheffield scored 125 for seven with four players hitting 25, including Rowbotham.

THE FIRST
RECORDED HUNDRED PARTNERSHIP

T. Sueter and G. Leer, Hampshire v Surrey at Broadhalfpenny Down, Hambledon, Hampshire, England. 1769.

The first recorded century partnership occurred in 1769 – it was 128 for the first wicket between Thomas Sueter and George Leer for Hampshire against Surrey.

THE FIRST
RECORDED HUNDRED

DUKE OF DORSET'S XI V WROTHAM AT DORSET, ENGLAND. THURSDAY 31 AUGUST 1769.

On the last day of August 1769, 16 days after the birth of Napoleon Bonaparte, the Duke of Dorset's XI played Wrotham. It was the first time a stroke by stroke scorecard of a match was kept. The match also featured the first known century when John Minshull, who batted at number three, scored 107. His Grace was obviously impressed by Minshull because, not long afterwards, he gave him a job as his gardener at a salary of eight shillings (about £25 today) a week.

THIS MATCH ALSO INCLUDED: The FIRST recorded stroke by stroke scorecard

THE LAST
BATSMAN TO USE A
BAT WIDER THAN THE WICKET

T. WHITE, CHERTSEY V HAMBLEDON AT LALEHAM BURWAY CRICKET
GROUND, SURREY, ENGLAND. MONDAY 23 SEPTEMBER 1771.

Playing for Chertsey against Hambledon, Thomas 'Shock' or 'Daddy' White (1740–1831) arrived at the wicket with a homemade bat wider than the stumps and took guard. There was no rule as to the width of a bat at that time but that did not stop protests from the Hambledon players. One of them produced a whittling knife and began to whittle down the bat until it was of a more normal size. White was said to be furious at the assault on his creation. Not long after the incident, the game's lawmakers decreed that a bat could not be more than 4½ inches (11.43 cm) wide. Currently, the bat can be no longer than 38 inches (96.5 cm) and no wider than 4¼ inches (10.79 cm).

THE FIRST
RECORDED USE OF
AN ATTACKING FIELD

ENGLAND V HAMPSHIRE AT SEVENOAKS VINE CRICKET CLUB GROUND,
THE VINE PAVILION, HOLLY BUSH LANE, SEVENOAKS, KENT, ENGLAND.
MONDAY 28 JUNE 1773.

The first recorded instance of an attacking field took place in a match between England and Hampshire at Sevenoaks Vine Cricket Club Ground. Hampshire made 77 in their first innings while England made 177, including 73 from Richard Miller. In their second innings Hampshire were all out for 49 but England opener Richard Simmons was told to field close in and so 'greatly intimidated the Hampshire gentlemen'. It worked, as England won by an innings and 51 runs.

THE FIRST
SIX-SEAMED BALL
PENSHURST, KENT, ENGLAND. 1775.

Reference to the first six-seamed ball is made in 1775 when Dukes, the family firm based in Penshurst, Kent, presented one to HRH the Prince of Wales (later King George IV). The first reference to the ball's colour – crimson – was made in 1753 in a poem about a match played on the ground at Sevenoaks Vine. The oldest surviving ball is now in the museum at Lord's. It dates from 1820 and was used in a match at the ground between MCC and Norfolk in which William Ward scored 278.

THE FIRST
USE OF THE THIRD STUMP
COULSDON CRICKET CLUB V CHERTSEY CRICKET CLUB AT LALEHAM BURWAY CRICKET GROUND, SURREY, ENGLAND. FRIDAY 6 SEPTEMBER 1776.

It is believed that the third stump was first used in a match in Surrey between Coulsdon and Chertsey. Chertsey had a bowler with the unusual name of Lumpy Stevens. He was so accurate that often his deliveries would pass through the two stumps, meaning that the batsman was not out because they and the single bail were untouched. This happened in a game in 1772 when Chertsey met Hambledon. Three times in a row Stevens bowled to Hambledon's ace batsman John Small and three times the ball passed between the two stumps. In 1774 a committee met to make revisions to the Laws of the game and one was the inclusion of a third stump. Although no scorecard exists for the game, historians believe that this was the birth of the third stump. The third stump became compulsory nine years later, although it was not until 1931 that final modifications were made to the size of the wicket. It is now 28 inches (71 cm) high and 9 inches (23 cm) wide and has been since 1931. In the 17th century, the stumps could be as much as 6 feet (1.83 m) wide but could be less than 1 foot (30 cm) high. By 1700 they were normally 2 feet (60 cm) wide and 1 foot (30 cm) high.

THE FIRST
RECORDED CAUGHT AND BOWLED
ENGLAND V HAMPSHIRE AT SEVENOAKS VINE CRICKET CLUB GROUND, THE VINE PAVILION, HOLLY BUSH LANE, SEVENOAKS, KENT, ENGLAND. THURSDAY 19 JUNE 1777.

The first recorded instance of a bowler being credited with a caught and bowled dismissal occurred in 1777. Richard Francis was caught and bowled by John Wood for 26 in Hampshire's first innings.

THE FIRST
MENTION OF TWO BAILS
MAIDSTONE, KENT, ENGLAND. 1786.

It was ten years after the introduction of the third stump that the first reference was made to two bails on the wicket. Previous wickets had carried just one bail although it could be several feet in length. In 1786 an unofficial version of the Laws of the game was published in Maidstone and it is here that first mention is made of two bails.

THE FIRST
MATCH PLAYED AT LORD'S
Middlesex v Essex at Lord's Old Ground, Dorset Square, Marylebone, Middlesex, England. Thursday 31 May 1787.

The first match played at Lord's was a one-day game between Middlesex and Essex. Middlesex batted first and were all out for 58 with James Boorman hitting 23 of the runs. Butcher of Essex picked up five wickets. Essex put themselves into a strong position scoring 130 with opener Richard Newman scoring the first fifty at Lord's (he was out for 51). Butcher picked up another five wickets in Middlesex's second innings but could not stop them making 203 – Boorman top scored again. Middlesex bowled Essex out for just 38 to win the match by 93 runs. In 1811 Thomas Lord moved his ground to Lisson Grove before relocating to the current site in 1814. Each time the turf was dug up and taken to the new venue.

THIS MATCH INCLUDED: The FIRST fifty at Lord's

THE FIRST
OVERSEAS TOUR PLANNED
Paris, France. Monday 10 August 1789.

John Frederick Sackville, 3rd Duke of Dorset was a devoted patron of cricket and responsible for a number of matches. In August 1789 he was the British ambassador in Paris and decided that it would be a good idea to further cement Anglo-French relations by arranging a goodwill cricket tour. He wrote to the Duke of Leeds, then Foreign Secretary and another cricketing enthusiast, to seek his assurances that the government would be supportive of the tour. Events overtook the tour and when the team arrived in Dover on 10 August 1789 ready for embarkation to Paris, they were met by the Duke of Dorset arriving post haste from the French capital, having fled the Revolution.

THIS WAS ALSO: The FIRST overseas tour cancelled for political reasons

THE FIRST
CRICKET ANNUAL
1791.

The most famous cricket annual, the yellow-jacketed *Wisden Cricketers' Almanack*, was not, as some might assume, the first cricket annual. That honour goes to Samuel Britcher who published his book in 1791. It contained the full scores for important matches for each season along with a selection of lesser games. In 1793 Britcher started publishing batting averages of the season. Britcher's was published annually until 1805. (See 1864, page 47.)

THE FIRST
CRICKET MATCH ON HORSEBACK
LINSTEAD PARK, KENT, ENGLAND. 6 MAY 1794.

There is almost no human activity that someone will not want to gamble on. In May 1794 two teams – the Gentlemen of the Hill and the Gentlemen of the Dale – took part in an equestrian game of cricket 'for one guinea [about £58 in today's terms] a man, the whole to be performed on horseback'. The players used long-handed bats for the game, which they had specially manufactured.

THE FIRST
LBW
THE HONOURABLE J. TUFTON, SURREY V XIII OF ENGLAND AT MOULSEY HURST, SURREY, ENGLAND. WEDNESDAY 12 AUGUST 1795.

On 12–15 August 1795 Surrey played XIII of England at Moulsey Hurst. The Honourable John Tufton became the first player given out leg before wicket. Batting at number three for the XIII of England, he is recorded in the scorebook as 'lbw b Wells 3'. Up to this time, lbws had been given as 'bowled'.

THE FIRST
MENTION OF CRICKET IN PRINT, AUSTRALIA
SYDNEY, AUSTRALIA. SUNDAY 8 JANUARY 1804.

Cricket was mentioned in print in Australia for the first time when, in 1804, the *Sydney Gazette and New South Wales Advertiser* reported, 'The late intense weather has been very favourable to the amateurs of cricket who have scarce lost a day for the last month.'

THE FIRST

MATCH FOR THE Bs

**THE BS V ENGLAND AT LORD'S OLD GROUND, DORSET SQUARE,
MARYLEBONE, MIDDLESEX, ENGLAND. MONDAY 8 JULY 1805.**

For a period between 1805 and 1837 the majority of the greatest players
in English cricket had surnames that began with B. Consequently, there
were arranged a dozen matches for The Bs against an assortment of
teams. The first began in the summer of 1805 at Lord's Old Ground. The
Bs batted first and made 100 all out before England made 126. The Bs
made 154 in their second knock and then dismissed England for 107 to
win by 21 runs. The Bs' team consisted of William Barton, Billy Beldham,
John Wells (unsurprisingly, given his name didn't start with a B, his only
appearance for The Bs. He got into the team through a family connection
– he was Billy Beldham's brother-in-law), George Beldham (his only First
Class match), James Bennett, Richard Beckett, Lord Frederick Beauclerk,
John Bennett, Henry Bentley, Samuel Bridger and Thomas Burgoyne. In
1817 The Bs beat England by 114 runs, in 1822 by seven wickets, in 1823
by an innings and 14 runs and in 1824 by 183 runs. In the match played
on 12, 13 and 14 June 1810 The Bs were bowled out for just six – the
lowest score in an important match. (See 1837, page 41.)

THE FIRST

RECORDED
ETON v HARROW MATCH

**Eton College v Harrow School, Lord's Old Ground, Dorset Square,
Marylebone, Middlesex, England. Friday 2 August 1805.**

Although cricket was played at Eton in the early part of the 18th century,
it was not until 1805 that the first match that we have definite details of
occurred. Lord Byron played for Harrow against Eton in the first match
at Lord's Old Ground despite being handicapped with a clubfoot. With the
help of a runner, Byron made seven in Harrow's first innings, out of a total
score of 55. Eton made 122 in their innings and Byron took one wicket,

bowling John Kaye for seven. Harrow were dismissed for 65 in their second innings and Byron made just two. Eton College won by an innings and two runs. In both innings Byron followed a pupil called Shakespear into bat. The match became an annual event from 1822 except in 1829–1831, 1856 and during the World Wars. In the late 19th and early 20th centuries the Eton-Harrow fixture was a key part of the London scene.

THE FIRST
GENTLEMEN v PLAYERS MATCH
LORD'S OLD GROUND, DORSET SQUARE, MARYLEBONE, MIDDLESEX, ENGLAND. MONDAY 7 JULY 1806.

Very little detail of the first match remains. The Players batted first and were all out for 69. Oddly, we know of only two bowlers who took wickets but we know who caught or, in one case, stumped the batsmen. The Gentlemen made 195 and again the catchers and the wicketkeeper are known but only one bowler. The Players were all out in their second innings for 112 and the only wicket for which we have complete details was one taken (bowled) by Lord Frederick Beauclerk, the son of the 5th Duke of St Albans. The Gentlemen won by an innings and 14 runs. The match was the highlight of the cricket season before the advent of Test matches. To be appointed the captain of the Players was considered a great accolade and Jack Hobbs had the honour 22 times. (See 1962, page 148.)

THE FIRST
RECORDED DOUBLE CENTURY
W. WARD, MCC V NORFOLK AT LORD'S CRICKET GROUND, ST JOHN'S WOOD ROAD, ST JOHN'S WOOD, MIDDLESEX, ENGLAND. MONDAY 24 JULY 1820.

William Ward became the first batsman to score a double century when he hit 278 of MCC's 473. MCC then bowled out Norfolk for 92 before they made 108 in their second innings. With three players absent hurt, Norfolk were bowled out for 72 as MCC won by 417 runs.

THE FIRST
RECORDED WIDES
1827.

Wides, which had been introduced in 1816, were first recorded in scorebooks from 1827 onwards. Prior to that, they were recorded as byes. In 1830 the first no-balls were recorded and in 1848 the first leg bye.

ALSO: The FIRST recorded no-balls • The FIRST recorded leg bye

THE FIRST
OXFORD UNIVERSITY v CAMBRIDGE UNIVERSITY
MATCH
LORD'S CRICKET GROUND, ST JOHN'S WOOD ROAD, ST JOHN'S WOOD, MIDDLESEX, ENGLAND. MONDAY 4 JUNE 1827.

Fourteen players made their First Class debuts in this Varsity match. Oxford batted first and made 258. The unusually named Rice Price was the top scorer with 71. Captain Herbert Jenner took five wickets although his full bowling analysis has been lost in the mists of time. Cambridge were dismissed for a disappointing 92 with Jenner leading the charge with 47. There was no play on the final day and the match was declared a draw. The match has been played annually since 1838 except when war has intervened. Cambridge captain Herbert Jenner was the last survivor of the match to die – he passed away on 30 July 1904, aged 98, having changed his name to Herbert Jenner-Fust in 1864. (See 1904, page 93.)

THE FIRST
MATCH IN AUSTRALIA FOR WHICH RECORDS SURVIVE
Sydney, Australia. 1830

Cricket was played regularly in Sydney in 1803 but no clubs were established until 1826. Civilians (76 and 136) beat 57th Regiment (101 and 87) by 24 runs on 26 February 1830 in the first match in Australia for which team scores survive. At stake was £20 (worth about £990 today) and around a hundred people watched the match, the first time the number of spectators had been mentioned in Australia. The first First Class match in Australia was not played until 11 February 1851, when Van Diemen's Land met Port Philip District of Victoria at Launceston. The first match between two mainland colonies was on 27 March 1856 . New South Wales (76 and 16 for seven) beat Victoria (63 and 28) by three wickets at Richmond Paddock, Melbourne Cricket Club's new ground, which was to become the modern-day Melbourne Cricket Ground.

THE FIRST
RECORDED COMPLETE BOWLING ANALYSIS
YORKSHIRE V NORFOLK AT HYDE PARK GROUND, SHEFFIELD, SOUTH YORKSHIRE, ENGLAND. MONDAY 14 JULY 1834.

The match between Yorkshire and Norfolk played at Sheffield is the first match for which we have existing complete bowling analyses including maiden overs.

THE FIRST
TEAM TO FOLLOW ON
LEFT-HANDED V RIGHT-HANDED AT LORD'S CRICKET GROUND, ST JOHN'S WOOD ROAD, ST JOHN'S WOOD, MIDDLESEX, ENGLAND. MONDAY 13 JULY 1835.

The Laws of cricket were changed on 20 May 1835 so that any team that was lagging 100 runs or more behind their opponents after their first innings was forced to bat again, or follow on. The first team forced to follow on were Left-Handed who scored 63 after Right-Handed hit them for 202. In their second innings they fared even worse and were dismissed for 52 giving Right-Handed a victory by an innings and 87 runs. The Law was modified in 1854.

THE FIRST
NORTH v SOUTH
MATCH

**NORTH V SOUTH AT LORD'S CRICKET GROUND, ST JOHN'S WOOD ROAD,
ST JOHN'S WOOD, MIDDLESEX, ENGLAND. MONDAY 11 JULY 1836.**

In the days before Test matches between Gentlemen and Players were popular with the public, the first (of 155) North v South match was held at Lord's. It is not known who won the first toss but South batted first and were all out for 97 with only two players making double figures. Fast bowler Thomas Barker took seven wickets and then opened the innings for North, scoring 25 of the total of 109. South slow bowler John Bayley picked up six wickets. When South batted again Barker picked up three more wickets to give him ten for the match as South made 69 all out. Barker was still at the crease for 12 not out when North reached 58 and won by six wickets. The match, scheduled for three days, ended in two.

Another match was played in 1836 and then again in 1837 and 1838 before the North v South match disappeared from the calendar until 1849 when it became virtually an annual event. Unlike many competitive matches, players could represent either side depending on where they were living at the time. (See 1961, page 147.)

THE LAST
MATCH FOR THE Bs

**The Bs v MCC at Lord's Cricket Ground, St John's Wood Road, St
John's Wood, Middlesex, England. Monday 31 July 1837.**

The last of the dozen matches for The Bs saw MCC batting first and they were all out for 76. The Bs then made 86. In their second innings MCC went one better than their first knock and scored 77 despite having two players absent hurt and one who retired not out. MCC then bowled out The Bs for 50 and they, too, had two players absent hurt. The last Bs team consisted of Edward Barnett, Thomas Box, Thomas Beagley, James Broadbridge, William Barnett, John Bayley, Robert Broughton, Roger Kynaston (he appeared for The Bs in place of Henry Broughton), Charles Barnett, Aubrey Beauclerk (son of Lord Frederick who played in the first match for the Bs in 1805) and Frederick Hervey-Bathurst. (See 1805, page 37.)

THE FIRST
REFERENCE TO SLEDGING
WEDNESDAY 7 FEBRUARY 1838.

The first reference to sledging appeared in the *Commercial Journal*, which noted that it was the 'low slang and insulting remarks so often resorted to by Australians'.

THE FIRST
RECORDED BATSMAN TO SCORE NINE RUNS FROM ONE BALL
THE HONOURABLE F.G.B. PONSONBY, MCC V CAMBRIDGE UNIVERSITY AT PARKER'S PIECE, CAMBRIDGE, ENGLAND. THURSDAY 19 MAY 1842.

The Honourable Frederick Ponsonby became the first recorded batsman to have scored nine runs from one ball while playing for MCC against Cambridge University at Parker's Piece, Cambridge. Cambridge University won the toss and decided to bat. They were bowled out for 169 while MCC made 197 in reply. Ponsonby scored 39 including one stroke for nine before he was bowled. Cambridge University made 110 in their second innings and, although set a small target, MCC struggled and were 83 for seven by the time they won the match by three wickets. Ponsonby was on nought not out.

THE FIRST
INTERNATIONAL OUTSIDE BRITAIN
UNITED STATES OF AMERICA V CANADA AT ST GEORGE'S CLUB GROUND, NEW YORK, UNITED STATES OF AMERICA. TUESDAY 24 SEPTEMBER 1844.

The first international match outside Britain was played in 1844 in New York between the United States and Canada. The United States won the toss and decided to field. Canada made 82 with Sheffield-born Sam Wright taking five wickets. Henry Groom took three wickets and he bowled the first ball to D. Winckworth. The USA scored 64, one more than Canada's second innings total. Groom took seven wickets. When bad weather prevented play on the second day, it was agreed to extend the match into a third day. The USA were dismissed for 58 in their second innings resulting in a Canadian win by 23 runs and they collected a $1,000 prize (roughly $30,000 today).

Four years earlier, Toronto and St George's of New York had played in the first match between teams from different countries. St George's won the match in New York by ten wickets. Players from both teams represented their respective countries in 1844.

THE ONLY
BOWLER TO TAKE ALL TEN WICKETS BOWLED
J. Wisden, North v South at Lord's Cricket Ground, St John's Wood Road, St John's Wood, Middlesex, England. Monday 15 July 1850.

The only cricketer to take all ten wickets bowled, as opposed to caught, in an important match was John Wisden, the founder of the eponymous almanack. Standing only 5 foot 4 inches (1.62 m) tall, the fast bowler was nicknamed 'The Little Wonder'. He was among the first cricketers, if not the first cricketer, to play wearing a straw hat rather than the white top hat more usually worn. Playing for the North, he bowled unchanged from the Pavilion End and it was said that his deliveries 'turned in a yard from the off'. (On 9 July 1835 Eton schoolboy John Kirwan took all ten wickets bowled in the second innings against MCC at Agar's Plough, Eton College.)

THE FIRST

BATSMAN GIVEN OUT HANDLED THE BALL IN FIRST CLASS CRICKET

J. Grundy, MCC v Kent at Lord's Cricket Ground, St John's Wood Road, St John's Wood, Middlesex, England. Monday 8 June 1857.

James Grundy became the first player in First Class cricket given out handled the ball while playing for MCC against Kent at Lord's. He had 15 on the board when he was given out. MCC won the match by five runs.

THE FIRST

BOWLER PRESENTED WITH A HAT FOR TAKING THREE CONSECUTIVE WICKETS

H.H. STEPHENSON, ALL ENGLAND XI V XXII OF HALLAM AND STAVELEY AT HYDE PARK GROUND, SHEFFIELD, SOUTH YORKSHIRE, ENGLAND. WEDNESDAY 8 SEPTEMBER 1858.

Playing for All England XI against the 22-man Hallam and Staveley at Hyde Park Ground, Sheffield captain Heathfield Stephenson was presented with a white hat after he took three consecutive wickets – the first instance of such a presentation being made to a bowler. This is the origin of the term 'hat-trick'.

All England XI batted first and were all out for 55 with Francis Tinley taking seven for 29. Hallam and Staveley were all out for 63 with only one player (Lieutenant Elmhirst) reaching double figures – he scored exactly ten. John Jackson took 12 for 25. All England XI's second innings was slightly better – they reached 107 all out with Tinley picking up another seven wickets, this time for the slightly less economical 38 runs conceded. When Hallam and Staveley batted they made 103 with Stephenson taking ten for 27. Hallam and Staveley won by one wicket.

THE FIRST

OVERSEAS TOUR BY AN ENGLISH TEAM

GEORGE PARR'S XI TO CANADA AND UNITED STATES OF AMERICA. SATURDAY 24 SEPTEMBER 1859 (FIRST MATCH).

The first overseas tour undertaken by an English team was one to Canada and the United States of America, captained by George Parr and organized by W.P. Pickering. Their first match was against Lower Canada at Montreal, Quebec. Lower Canada fielded 22 players and in their first innings were dismissed for 85 with J.G. Daly being the only player to reach double figures – he was bowled by George Parr for 19. John Jackson of Nottinghamshire took seven for 21; Billy Caffyn of Kent took five for 33 while Parr himself bowled 11 overs, including five maidens, and returned six wickets for eight runs. Parr also top scored in his team's total of 117, reaching 24. F. Fisher took five for 53. The 22-man Lower Canada team made 63 in their second innings and only J.U. Smith reached double figures – he was bowled by Parr, who picked up ten wickets for 19 runs. George Parr's XI made their target, reaching 32 for two to win by eight wickets. Parr's team played two games in Canada, winning them both, and three matches in America, easily winning all three, two by an innings margin.

THE FIRST

TOUR BY AN ENGLISH TEAM
TO AUSTRALIA

H.H. STEPHENSON'S XI TO AUSTRALIA. WEDNESDAY 1 JANUARY 1862 (FIRST MATCH).

Fifteen years before the first official Test match, an English team, captained by H.H. Stephenson, who also kept wicket, and organized by Spiers and Pond, travelled to Australia where they played a dozen matches, winning six, drawing four and losing just two. Interestingly, the matches between Stephenson's team and the Australian colonies were referred to as test matches. The first of these test matches occurred on New Year's Day when

XVIII of Victoria met H.H. Stephenson's XI. Victoria won the toss and decided to bat. They were dismissed for 118 and captain George Marshall, who had been born in Nottingham, England, was the top scorer with 27. 'Farmer' Bennett took seven for 53 and George Griffith took seven for 30. H.H. Stephenson's XI scored 305 .The highest scorer was Billy Caffyn of Kent, who had been on the first overseas tour (see above, page 45), with 79. XVIII of Victoria fared even worse in their second innings and were dismissed for 91. Tom Sewell took seven for 20. H.H. Stephenson's XI won by an innings and 96 runs.

THE FIRST
FIRST CLASS MATCH IN NEW ZEALAND
OTAGO V CANTERBURY AT SOUTH DUNEDIN RECREATION GROUND, DUNEDIN, NEW ZEALAND.
WEDNESDAY 27 JANUARY 1864.

The first First Class match in New Zealand was played between Otago and Canterbury. Canterbury won the toss and decided to field. Otago were all out for 78. Top scorer was James Fulton who hit 25. For Canterbury R. Taylor took six wickets for 21. Canterbury were all out for 34 and George Sale was the only batsman not to score. Otago made 74 in their second innings and then bowled Canterbury out for 42 with F. MacDonald taking six for 17. Otago won by 76 runs. Seventeen players made their First Class debuts in the match but five of the Otago team had previously appeared in First Class matches for Victoria. Oddly, six-ball overs were used for the first innings and four-ball ones for the second.

THE FIRST
LEGAL USE OF OVER-ARM BOWLING
Friday 10 June 1864.

Over-arm bowling was legalized in cricket on 10 June 1864. When the sport began, bowlers rolled the ball underarm, as in Crown Green Bowls, and the batsman stood still and hit the approaching ball, much like a golfer hits the ball in his game. It was not until 1744 that bowlers began to lob the ball and by 1773 bowling to length had become the norm. However, in 1816 a new rule outlawed all but underarm bowling 'with the hand below the elbow... if the ball be jerked or the arm extended from the body horizontally... the Umpire shall call "No Ball".'

The style of bowling round-arm was popularized by John Willes of Kent who batted against his sister Christina who, because of her voluminous skirts, was forced to bowl round-armed to him. He opened the bowling round-armed for Kent in a match at Lord's against the MCC on 15 July 1822 and was the first player no-balled for throwing. He refused to participate in the match and left the ground 'in high dudgeon'. On 26 August 1862, opening England's bowling against Surrey at The Oval, Edgar Willsher was the first bowler no-balled for bowling over-arm by umpire John Lillywhite. Willsher was no-balled six times but he refused to change his style and the England team left the field in solidarity, causing the abandonment of play for the day. The next day Umpire Lillywhite stood firm in his decision that Willsher should not be allowed to bowl over-arm and was replaced as umpire. Without the constant no-balling Willsher took six for 49.

JOHN WILLES WAS: The **FIRST** player no-balled for throwing.
EDGAR WILLSHER WAS: The **FIRST** bowler no-balled for bowling over-arm

THE FIRST
EDITION OF WISDEN CRICKETERS' ALMANACK
2 NEW COVENTRY STREET, HAYMARKET, LONDON, ENGLAND. 1864.

The bible of cricket was first published by the former English cricketer John Wisden (1826–1884) in 1864, a year after he retired, and was originally known as *The Cricketer's Almanack*. Wisden wanted the book to compete with Fred Lillywhite's *The Guide To Cricketers*. The first edition was only 112 pages long and cost one shilling (just over £2 in today's terms). As well as cricket, it contained the dates of battles in the English Civil War, an account of the trial of King Charles I, the winners of The Oaks, the Derby and St Leger, lengths of British canals, the results of the Boat race and the rules of quoiting.

From 1866 it began to include full scores of the previous season's important matches and the following year it had 'Births and deaths of cricketers'. In 1887 it contained batting and bowling averages from the previous season and a fixture list for the forthcoming one. Five years later, its first obituaries appeared. From the sixth edition, it became known as *Wisden Cricketers' Almanack*, although the yellow jackets did not appear until the 75th edition in 1938. Previously, its covers had varied between yellow, buff and pink. The 75th edition was also the first to display on its cover the woodcut of two Victorian cricketers by Eric Ravilious.

The book has had just 16 editors in more than 140 years of publication. Its Cricketers of the Year tradition began in 1889 with the naming of Six Great Bowlers of the Year. Usually, five players are selected annually although there have been some surprising omissions. Abdul Qadir, Bishan Bedi, Wes Hall, Inzamam-ul-Haq and Jeff Thomson, in particular, were never honoured.

<hr>

THE FIRST
INTER-COLONIAL MATCH
IN THE WEST INDIES
BARBADOS V DEMERARA AT GARRISON SAVANNAH, BRIDGETOWN, BARBADOS. THURSDAY 16 FEBRUARY 1865.

The first inter-colonial match in the West Indies was a contest between Barbados and Demerara – it was also the only First Class match played at Garrison Savannah, Bridgetown. Barbados batted first and were all out for 74 with fast bowler George Whitehall the top scorer on 21. Only one other player reached double figures. Frederick Smith took six Demeraran wickets as they were all out for 22. Captain G.H. Oliver was the top scorer with eight runs, closely followed by Extras on seven. Frederick Smith opened Barbados's second innings and hit the nation's first First Class fifty (and was the first player to carry his bat) as they made 124 and then picked up four more wickets as Demerara were all out for 38. Barbados enjoyed a sweet victory by 138 runs.

THE FIRST
FULL TOUR OF ENGLAND BY AN OVERSEAS TEAM

ENGLAND. MONDAY 25 MAY–SATURDAY 17 OCTOBER 1868.

The first overseas team to visit England was made up entirely of Australian Aborigines. Between May and October they played 47 games, winning 14, losing 14 and drawing 19. The tour was organized by former Middlesex and Surrey all-rounder Charles Lawrence, who also captained and managed the team. Their tour uniform consisted of white flannels, red Garibaldi shirts with blue sashes and ties. As well as playing cricket, they were also called upon to demonstrate aboriginal skills including spear and boomerang throwing as well as running, hurdling, the long jump and a race carrying water buckets.

The 13 tourists were given nicknames to make them more acceptable to the English public: Bullocky (Bullchanach), Charley Dumas (Pripumuarraman), Cuzens (Zellanach), Dick-a-Dick (Jungunjinanuke), Jim Crow (Jallachmurrimin), King Cole (Brippokei), Mosquito (Grongarrong), Mullagh (Unaarrimin), Peter (Arrahmunijarrimum), Red Cap (Brimbunyah), Sundown (Ballrinjarrimin), Tiger (Bonnibarngeet) and Twopenny (Murrumgunarriman). The tour was extremely arduous and only ten of the original 13 completed it. King Cole died of tuberculosis in Guy's Hospital, London, on 24 June. Sundown and Jim Crow returned to Australia in August, two months before their team-mates. Red Cap and Tiger played in all 47 matches.

THE FIRST

RECORDED BATSMAN
TO SCORE A TRIPLE AND THEN QUADRUPLE CENTURY

E.F.S. TYLECOTE, CLASSICAL V MODERN AT CLIFTON COLLEGE CLOSE GROUND, 32 COLLEGE ROAD, CLIFTON, BRISTOL, GLOUCESTERSHIRE, ENGLAND. TUESDAY 26 MAY 1868.

Born at Marston Mortain Rectory, Ampthill, Bedfordshire, on 23 June 1849, Edward Tylecote was the son of the Reverend Canon T. Tylecote. He played for the Clifton College from 1864 until 1868 and was captain in his last year. He became the first man to score a known triple and then quadruple century when he hit 404 for Classical against Modern at Clifton College. The Moderns batted first and scored 100. Tylecote took three wickets. Tylecote opened for the Classicals and the innings lasted six hours over three afternoons (from 3 pm to 5.30 pm). The next highest score was 52. Tylecote scored one seven, five fives, 21 fours, 39 threes, 42 twos and 87 ones, all of which were run except for one four hit out of the ground.

He went up to St John's College, Oxford, and played cricket for Oxford from 1869 until 1872, winning his blue all four years, and being captain in his last two years. He played 93 First Class matches and six Test matches. He became a schoolmaster at the Royal Military Academy, Woolwich in 1875 and stayed there for 20 years. He later taught at a number of preparatory schools and became a keen lepidopterist. He died at New Hunstanton, Norfolk, on 15 March 1938.

THE FIRST

BATSMAN TO SCORE A FIRST CLASS CENTURY
BEFORE LUNCH ON THE FIRST DAY

W.G. Grace, MCC v Kent at St Lawrence Ground, Old Dover Road, Canterbury, Kent, England. Wednesday 11 August 1869.

The Grand Old Man was the first to score a century before lunch on the first day of a First Class match. By the time the luncheon interval was called, Grace was on 116 not out. He moved his score on to 127 before George 'Farmer' Bennett caught him off the bowling of Edgar Willsher. MCC made 449 and won by an innings and 88 runs. Each side fielded 12 players.

THE ONLY
FATAL ACCIDENT IN ENGLISH FIRST CLASS CRICKET

G. SUMMERS, NOTTINGHAMSHIRE V MCC AT LORD'S CRICKET GROUND, ST JOHN'S WOOD ROAD, ST JOHN'S WOOD, MIDDLESEX, ENGLAND. WEDNESDAY 15 JUNE 1870.

Popular Nottinghamshire batsman George Summers died on 19 June 1870, aged 25, four days after being struck on the head at Lord's by a quick delivery from John Platts, an MCC staffer, making his debut in First Class cricket. The pitch had not been properly prepared and the ball bounced around at head-height in many deliveries. Summers was put in a carriage and taken over rough roads to his father's house in Nottingham, where he died. Shaken by what had happened, Platts never bowled fast again and concentrated his efforts on medium pace where he achieved some success.

FATAL BALL

On 17 January 1959 Karachi wicketkeeper Abdul Aziz died aged just 18 after being struck in the chest by a ball from Dildar Awan while playing against Combined Services in the final of Quaid-e-Azam Trophy at Karachi Parsi Institute Ground. He retired hurt, collapsed and died on the way to hospital. Just a week earlier he had been Hanif Mohammad's partner when the batsman scored a record-breaking 499 in the semi final against Bahawalpur.

THE FIRST

PLAYER TO SCORE
2,000 FIRST CLASS RUNS IN
THE SAME SEASON

W.G. Grace, 1871.

In 1871 Grace scored 2,739 First Class runs, the first player to break the 2,000-run milestone. That year he also became the first player to score ten First Class centuries in a season. It would not be until 1978–1979 that a player would score ten centuries in an overseas season.

W.G GRACE WAS ALSO: The FIRST player to score ten First Class centuries in a season

---

THE FIRST
COUNTY BATSMAN GIVEN OUT
HANDLED THE BALL

G. Bennett, Kent v Sussex at County Ground, Eaton Road, Hove, West Sussex, England. Tuesday 13 August 1872.

George 'Farmer' Bennett of Kent playing against Sussex at the County Ground, Hove became the first county batsman given out handled the ball. He was still on nought when he removed a ball that had lodged in his clothing. In 1899 Law 33(b) was introduced which declared the ball dead in those circumstances.

THE FIRST
TIED FIRST CLASS MATCH IN NEW ZEALAND

WELLINGTON V NELSON AT BASIN RESERVE, WELLINGTON, NEW ZEALAND. WEDNESDAY 18 MARCH 1874.

The first tied First Class match in New Zealand occurred between Wellington and Nelson at Basin Reserve, Wellington. Eighteen players made their First Class debuts in the match. The home side won the toss and scored 63 and 118. They dismissed Nelson for 111 (!) and 70 with Isaac Salmon taking a hat-trick in his second First Class match and ending with figures of seven for 36 from 22 five-ball overs. The next, and so far only other, tied match happened 103 years, ten months and 16 days later when England XI played Central Districts at Pukekura Park, New Plymouth.

THE FIRST
PLAYER TO DO THE DOUBLE -
1,000 RUNS AND 100 WICKETS
IN SAME SEASON
W.G. Grace, 1874.

In 1874 W.G. Grace scored 1,664 runs and took 140 wickets to become the first cricketer to achieve the double in a First Class season. It was a feat he repeated for the next four seasons but it was not until 1882 that another player, C.T. Studd, managed to equal the achievement.

THE FIRST
BATSMAN TO SCORE A
FIRST CLASS CENTURY
WITHOUT ANY BOUNDARIES
A.W. Ridley, Hampshire v Kent at Mount Field, St Ann's, Faversham, Kent, England. Thursday 17 August 1876.

Arthur Ridley scored 104 for Hampshire against Kent in an innings total of 277. The second highest scorer was Extras with 48. His knock included 14 threes, 15 twos and 32 singles. The match was a remarkable effort for Ridley who took five wickets in each innings – five for 52 and five for 61 – as Hampshire won by an innings and six runs. Those wishing to see where this remarkable event occurred will be disappointed as the ground was largely built on in the 1930s and only a small strip of land survives as part of the King George V Playing Fields.

THE FIRST

TEST MATCH

**Australia v England at Melbourne Cricket Ground, Jolimont,
Melbourne, Victoria, Australia. Thursday 15 March 1877.**

After Dave Gregory, the captain of Australia, tossed the coin and James
Lillywhite, his England opposite number, called incorrectly, Gregory
decided to bat first and thus the first Test match began. On a sunny
autumn Thursday at 1.05 pm 34-year-old Alfred Shaw of Nottinghamshire
bowled to Charles Bannerman, a 25-year-old Kentish man playing his
tenth First Class innings. Bannerman scored the first run in Test cricket
off Shaw's second delivery. Before a 40-minute luncheon interval was
taken at 2 pm, Allen Hill bowled Nat Thompson for one to take the first
Test wicket. Hill also took the first catch in Test history when he held Tom
Horan off Shaw's bowling. Bannerman scored the first Test century (taking
160 minutes) on the first day, which closed at 5 pm with Australia on 166
for six with Bannerman not out on 126 and Blackham not out on three.
Edward Gregory was the first player out for a duck in a Test, being caught
by Andrew Greenwood off Lillywhite's bowling.

On the second day play began at 1.45 pm and Bannerman retired hurt
just after lunch on 165, having been at the crease for four hours and 45
minutes, hitting 18 fours. It was his only First Class century. Australia were
finally bowled out for 245 with Bannerman contributing 67 per cent of the
runs, the highest individual contribution to any Test innings. No other
Australian made more than 20. England made 196 with Billy Midwinter
becoming the first player to take five Test wickets in an innings – five for
78 – before they skittled out Australia for 104. Despite needing just 154
for victory, England's second innings collapsed and they lost the match by
45 runs.

**THIS MATCH WAS ALSO: The FIRST coin toss in a Test match
• The FIRST Test delivery • The FIRST Test run • The FIRST
Test wicket • The FIRST Test catch • The FIRST Test duck
• The FIRST Test century • The FIRST batsman to retire hurt
in Test cricket • The FIRST player to take five Test wickets
in an innings**

ONE HUNDRED YEARS LATER

The scorecard of the first Test match did not appear in *Wisden Cricketers' Almanack* until 1977 when it accompanied coverage of the Centenary Test. Oddly, Australia won that match by 45 runs as well.

THE FIRST

TEST VICTORY FOR ENGLAND

ENGLAND V AUSTRALIA AT MELBOURNE CRICKET GROUND, JOLIMONT, MELBOURNE, VICTORIA, AUSTRALIA. WEDNESDAY 4 APRIL 1877.

England won their first Test match – the second Test match ever – having lost the toss. It was a low-scoring match. Australia batted first and scored 122 while England hit 261 (George Ulyett scored 52). Australia scored 259 in their second knock and England scampered to victory by four wickets, thanks to a second innings 63 from Ulyett.

THE FIRST

TEST HAT-TRICK

F.R. SPOFFORTH, AUSTRALIA V ENGLAND AT MELBOURNE CRICKET GROUND, JOLIMONT, MELBOURNE, VICTORIA, AUSTRALIA. THURSDAY 2 JANUARY 1879.

It was during the third Test match between the two old enemies that Fred Spofforth took the first hat-trick, dismissing Vernon Royle, Francis McKinnon and Tom Emmett, as England collapsed to 26 for seven. Australia won the match by ten wickets. 'Demon' Spofforth also became the first bowler to take ten wickets in a Test match when he claimed six for 48 and seven for 62 for a total of 13 for 110.

THIS MATCH ALSO INCLUDED: The FIRST bowler to take ten wickets in a Test match

THE FIRST
PLAYER TO CAPTAIN ENGLAND ON DEBUT

4TH LORD HARRIS, ENGLAND V AUSTRALIA AT MELBOURNE CRICKET GROUND, JOLIMONT, MELBOURNE, VICTORIA, AUSTRALIA. THURSDAY 2 JANUARY 1879.

George Robert Canning Harris, 4th Baron Harris, made his first appearance as England captain on his Test debut in the third contest between the two countries. He won two of his four Tests as English captain, losing one and drawing the other. He was unbeaten on English soil when he led the team. He also became involved in politics and was Under-Secretary of State for India from 25 June 1885, then Parliamentary Under-Secretary of State for War from 4 August 1886 to 1890 in the Conservative Government. He served as Governor of the Presidency of Bombay in British India from 1890 to 1895. He made his last First Class appearance for Kent against Surrey on 4 July 1911 against All-India at Catford when he was 60 years 151 days old. (See above, page 55.)

THIS MATCH ALSO INCLUDED: The FIRST peer to captain England

THE FIRST
BOWLER TO TAKE FOUR CONSECUTIVE WICKETS IN AUSTRALIA

G. ULYETT, LORD HARRIS'S ENGLISH XI V NEW SOUTH WALES AT ASSOCIATION GROUND, SYDNEY, NEW SOUTH WALES, AUSTRALIA. MONDAY 10 FEBRUARY 1879.

George Ulyett, playing for Lord Harris's English XI against New South Wales on a rain-soaked Association Ground pitch at Sydney, became the first bowler to take four wickets in consecutive balls in First Class cricket in Australia – dismissing Edwin Evans, Edwin Tindall, captain Dave Gregory and Fred Spofforth. New South Wales were all out for 49 in their second innings and, indeed, lost their last five wickets without troubling the scorers. Ulyett took four for 13 and Lord Harris's XI won by an innings and 41 runs.

THE FIRST
TEST CRICKETER TO DIE

J. SOUTHERTON, MITCHAM, SURREY, ENGLAND. WEDNESDAY 16 JUNE 1880.

James Southerton, an off-break round-arm bowler, made his debut in his first Test aged 49 years, 119 days – the oldest novice Test player. Southerton began playing as a batsman before becoming a slow round-arm bowler. In 1867 he played for three counties, Hampshire, Surrey and Sussex, but played most of his First Class cricket (286 matches) for Surrey. He died aged 53, just three years after his first Test match, but since the games were not designated as such until later, he died not knowing about his Test career.

THE FIRST
TEST MATCH IN ENGLAND

ENGLAND V AUSTRALIA AT THE OVAL, KENNINGTON, SURREY, ENGLAND. MONDAY 6 SEPTEMBER 1880.

It was the fourth Test match played between the two countries and England fielded eight debutants, including W.G. Grace and his brothers Edward Mills – who faced the first ball and opened the batting with W.G. – and George Fredrick. The match had originally been intended as Surrey playing Australia but club secretary Charles Alcock was instrumental in arranging the first Test match in England instead.

On his Test debut William Gilbert Grace became the first player to score a century for England and the first on a Test debut. He made 152 before he was out as England were bowled out for 420. W.G. Grace and Lucas

---

THE FA CUP CONNECTION

Charles Alcock, educated at Harrow, was also secretary of the Football Association from 1870 until 1895 and, on 20 July 1871, suggested, 'That it is desirable that a Challenge Cup should be established in connection with the Association, for which all clubs belonging to the Association should be invited to compete.' This became the FA Cup, the world's oldest football competition, and Alcock captained the winning team, Wanderers, in the first Final in 1872. He scored the first disallowed goal in an FA Cup Final. He also refereed the Finals in 1875 and 1879. On 6 March 1875 he captained England against Scotland, scoring a goal in a 2-2 draw.

---

shared the first century partnership (120 for the second wicket). Australia made 149 in reply and captain Lord Harris enforced the follow-on. In their second knock, the Aussies made 327 but England struggled, despite needing just 56 for victory. They reached 57 with the loss of five wickets to win.

THIS MATCH WAS ALSO: The FIRST Test century for England • The FIRST Test century on debut for England • The FIRST Test century for England in England • The ONLY Englishman to score a century against Australia in England on debut • The FIRST hundred partnership in a Test match

———•••••———

THE ONLY
CABINET MINISTER TO PLAY CRICKET AND FOOTBALL FOR ENGLAND

THE HONOURABLE ALFRED LYTTELTON, ENGLAND V SCOTLAND AT THE OVAL, KENNINGTON, SURREY, ENGLAND. SATURDAY 3 MARCH 1877; ENGLAND V AUSTRALIA AT THE OVAL, KENNINGTON, SURREY, ENGLAND. MONDAY 6 SEPTEMBER 1880.

Alfred Lyttelton (1857–1913) was the eighth son and youngest of the 12 children of the 4th Baron Lyttelton and Mary Glynne, who was William Gladstone's sister-in-law. At Eton Lyttelton excelled in all sports, leading a friend to comment, 'No athlete was ever quite such an athlete, and no boyish hero was ever quite such a hero as was Alfred Lyttelton.' In 1875 he went up to Trinity College, Cambridge where he was the leading cricketer. He played just once for England at football, scoring his country's solitary goal in a 3-1 defeat against Scotland. He was amateur royal tennis champion from 1882–1896. He played in four Tests and his best bowling figures were four for 19, with underarm lobs.

He was Liberal Unionist MP for Warwick and Leamington from 1895 to 1906, when he lost his seat. Lyttelton represented St George's Hanover Square from June 1906 until his death. He served in the Cabinet as Secretary of State for the Colonies from 1903 until 1905. Lyttelton died on 5 July 1913, aged 56, in a nursing home at 3 Devonshire Terrace, Marylebone, London, from an abscess caused by being hit in the stomach while scoring 89 in a cricket match at Bethnal Green.

ALFRED LYTTELTON WAS ALSO: The FIRST player to represent England at football and cricket • The FIRST double international at football and cricket

THE FIRST
TEST PLAYER DISMISSED
FOR A PAIR

G.F. Grace, England v Australia at The Oval, Kennington, Surrey, England. Wednesday 8 September 1880.

The first Test match in England was held at The Oval and three Grace brothers made their Test debuts. W.G. and E.M. became the first brothers to open the batting for England. Only W.G. really shone, scoring 152 and taking three wickets (see 1880, page 57). E.M. scored 36 and nought, while George Frederick had the misfortune to become the first player in Test cricket to bag a pair – he was caught by Charles Bannerman off William Moule's bowling in the first innings when he batted at number nine and was clean bowled by Palmer when he opened England's second knock.

THIS MATCH ALSO INCLUDED: The FIRST brothers to open the batting for England

THE FIRST

PLAYER TO PLAY FOR AND AGAINST AUSTRALIA IN TEST MATCHES

W.E. MIDWINTER, AUSTRALIA V ENGLAND AT MELBOURNE CRICKET GROUND, JOLIMONT, MELBOURNE, VICTORIA, AUSTRALIA. THURSDAY 15 MARCH 1877; ENGLAND V AUSTRALIA AT MELBOURNE CRICKET GROUND, JOLIMONT, MELBOURNE, VICTORIA, AUSTRALIA. SATURDAY 31 DECEMBER 1881.

William Evans Midwinter was born at Lower Meend, St Briavels, Gloucestershire on 19 June 1851 and emigrated Down Under with his family in 1860. He made his Test debut for Australia in the inaugural match in 1877, scoring five and 17 and taking five for 78 off 54 overs in the first innings and one for 23 off 19 overs in the second. Returning to England, he played for Gloucestershire where he stayed until 1882. He was selected to play for England against Australia on the 1881–1882 tour and scored 40 in the Test, which began on 31 December 1881. Billy Midwinter played in all four Tests against Australia on that tour but, a year later, was back in Australia's green cap playing against England. In all he played in a dozen Tests, eight for Australia against England and four for England against Australia. He went mad with grief after the death of his wife and two children, and died aged 39 at Kew Insane Asylum, Princess Street and Yarra Boulevard, Kew, Melbourne, Victoria on 3 December 1890.

THE FIRST

FORMER TEST CRICKETER TO UMPIRE IN A TEST MATCH

J. LILLYWHITE, AUSTRALIA V ENGLAND AT MELBOURNE CRICKET GROUND, JOLIMONT, MELBOURNE, VICTORIA, AUSTRALIA. SATURDAY 31 DECEMBER 1881.

James Lillywhite became the first former Test cricketer to umpire in a Test match. Lillywhite had been England's captain in the first two Test matches. This match in which he umpired was a draw.

THE ONLY
COUNTY SIDE TO STRIKE
Nottinghamshire. 1881

Seven members of Nottinghamshire's First XI went on strike for most of the summer of 1881 in a protest against the county committee. The players wanted parity of pay and a guaranteed benefit after ten years' service. The strike was settled amicably the following year.

THE FIRST
WICKETKEEPER TO STUMP
BOTH OPENERS IN SAME TEST INNINGS
J.M. BLACKHAM, AUSTRALIA V ENGLAND AT MELBOURNE CRICKET GROUND, JOLIMONT, MELBOURNE, VICTORIA, AUSTRALIA. TUESDAY 3 JANUARY 1882.

Australia's Jack Blackham became the first wicketkeeper to stump both openers in the same innings in a Test match when he claimed the scalps of England's Dick Barlow and George Ulyett in the first Test, held at Melbourne. The feat would not be repeated in Australia until 1998–1999 when Ian Healey dismissed Mark Butcher and Alec Stewart.

THE FIRST
PLAYER TO CAPTAIN ENGLAND
AT CRICKET AND RUGBY
A.N. HORNBY, ENGLAND V AUSTRALIA AT THE OVAL, KENNINGTON, SURREY, ENGLAND. MONDAY 28 AUGUST 1882; ENGLAND V SCOTLAND AT WHALLEY RANGE, MANCHESTER, LANCASHIRE, ENGLAND. SATURDAY 4 MARCH 1882.

Albert Neilson Hornby was the sixth son of William Henry Hornby, the MP for Blackburn, 1857–1869. Known as 'Monkey' because he was short, he was captain of Lancashire for 20 years but was unable to replicate his county form on the international stage. He made just 21 runs in his three Tests with an average of 3.50 and a highest score of nine (compared to a top score of 188 for Lancashire) when he opened the second innings with W.G. Grace. He was captain when England lost the only Test of 1882, the Test that led to the Ashes. He made his Test debut for England at rugby on 5 February 1877 against Ireland in the first 15-a-side international. Coincidentally, the match was played at The Oval.

Five years later, he captained England at Manchester against Scotland in the Calcutta Cup. Scotland won the match by two tries. At the age of 35, he was rather old a sportsman when he achieved this feat and it was his last rugby Test. He won nine caps for England at rugby, playing club rugby for Preston Grasshoppers and Manchester. He also played football for Blackburn Rovers.

MY DEAR VICTORIOUS STOD

The only other man to captain England at cricket and rugby was Andrew Stoddart. He did not have a happy life and on Easter Saturday 3 April 1915, beset by money worries, in failing health and with an unhappy marriage, Stoddart shot himself in the head, in a bedroom at his home, 115 Clifton Hill, St John's Wood, London. Born at 10 Wellington Terrace, Westoe, South Shields, 'Stod' did not begin playing cricket until he was 22 when, in 1885, he made his debut for Middlesex. He toured Australia four times (twice as captain, including a winning tour in 1894–1895) and America and West Indies once each. In his 15-year career he scored 16,738 First Class runs including 26 centuries. From 1886 to 1893 he took part in ten international rugby matches as a three-quarter. He played in 16 Tests for England scoring 996 runs, which included two centuries. *Punch* celebrated the Ashes win in 1894–1895 with a poem, which contained the lines:

Then wrote the queen of England
Whose hand is blessed by God
I must do something handsome
For my dear victorious Stod.

THE FIRST
RECORDED MENTION
OF THE ASHES

The Sporting Times, London, England. Saturday 2 September 1882.

In the only Test of 1882 Australia beat England for the first time in England albeit by just seven runs. There were 39,194 spectators at the match, one of whom one died of a heart attack and another bit through the handle of his umbrella during the final stages. On 2 September a mock obituary appeared in *The Sporting Times*, written by Reginald Brooks under the pseudonym 'Bloobs' that read:

In Affectionate Remembrance

of

ENGLISH CRICKET,

which died at the Oval

on

29th AUGUST, 1882,

Deeply lamented by a large circle of sorrowing

friends and acquaintances

R.I.P.

N.B. – The body will be cremated and the

ashes taken to Australia

Some weeks after the end of the cricket season, an England team captained by the Honourable Ivo Bligh set off to tour Australia. Bligh told the press that he would 'return with the Ashes' but the term 'the Ashes' did not catch on until almost the turn of the century. On Christmas Eve 1882 at a social gathering in Sunbury, Victoria, Australia, some female guests gave Bligh a 6-inch (15-cm) high terracotta urn, containing some ashes, as a memento of his visit. It was probably a perfume jar and intended as a personal gift to Bligh rather than as a sporting trophy. A bag was later made in which to keep the urn and presented to Bligh in February 1883. Bligh kept the urn and bag at his home when the tourists returned home from Down Under.

In 1899, the Ashes were mentioned in the autobiography of Australian Test player George Giffen. Four years later, the press began using the term when England captain Pelham Warner said that he would 'regain the

Ashes'. The first mention of The Ashes in *Wisden Cricketers' Almanack* was in 1905, while *Wisden*'s first account of the legend did not occur until the 1922 edition. On 10 April 1927, Ivo Bligh (by then the 8th Earl of Darnley) died, aged 68, and his widow gave the original urn to the MCC.

There is some dispute as to what the urn contains. Various theories include the ashes of a stump, a bail, part of a ball or even a wedding veil. However, on 25 November 2006 an MCC spokesman said that it was '95 per cent' certain that the urn contains the ashes of a cricket bail.

—••••—

THE FIRST
FAMILY TO PROVIDE SEVEN FIRST CLASS CRICKETING BROTHERS

J. WALKER (1846–1868); A. WALKER (1846–1860); F. WALKER (1849–1860); A.H. WALKER (1855–1862); V.E. WALKER (1856–1877); R.D. WALKER (1861–1878) AND I.D. WALKER (1882–1884).

The first family to provide seven First Class cricketing brothers was the Walkers. The dates above refer to the extent of their First Class careers. Only four brothers ever appeared in the same team together.

John was born at Palmers Green, Middlesex on 15 September 1826 and appeared in 87 top-level matches, scoring 1,355 runs (top score 98) for Cambridge University, MCC and Middlesex. He died at Arnos Grove, Middlesex on 14 August 1885. Alfred was born at Southgate, Middlesex on 8 September 1827 and played 14 First Class matches, scoring 95 runs with a top score of 20 for Cambridge University and Middlesex. He died at Arnos Grove, Middlesex on 4 September 1870. Frederic was born at Southgate, Middlesex on 4 December 1829 and played 34 First Class matches, scoring 726 (top score 71) for Cambridge University, MCC and Middlesex. He died on 20 December 1889 at Arnos Grove, Middlesex.

Arthur Henry was born at Southgate, Middlesex on 30 June 1833 and played for MCC and Middlesex. He played 23 First Class matches and scored 601 runs with a top score of 90. He died on 4 October 1878 at Arnos Grove, Middlesex. Vyell Edward was born at Southgate, Middlesex on 20 April 1837. An underam slow right-hand bowler, he played for MCC and Middlesex in 145 games scoring 3,384 runs with a top score of 108. He was Middlesex captain from 1864 until 1872. He died at Arnos Grove, Middlesex on 3 January 1906. Russell Donnithorne was born at Southgate, Middlesex on 13 February 1842 and was a right-arm round-arm slow bowler for Oxford University, Middlesex and MCC. He played in 122 games, hitting 3,840 runs with a top score of 104. He died on 29 March 1922 at home in Regent's Park, London.

The final brother was Isaac Donnithorne who was born at Southgate, Middlesex on 8 January 1844. He played 294 First Class matches, scoring 11,400 runs with a top score of 179. He was a right-arm underarm slow bowler for Middlesex and MCC and also occasionally kept wicket. He was captain of Harrow from 1862 until 1863 and skipper of Middlesex from 1873 until 1884. He took 218 wickets at a cost of 4,755 runs and his best figures were six for 42. He died on 6 July 1898, aged 54, at his brother Russell's home in Regent's Park, London.

THE FIRST
TEST MATCH STAGED AT LORD'S

ENGLAND V AUSTRALIA AT LORD'S CRICKET GROUND, ST JOHN'S WOOD ROAD, ST JOHN'S WOOD, MIDDLESEX, ENGLAND. MONDAY 21 JULY 1884.

Lord's staged its first Test match and London became the only city to have two grounds in regular current use for Tests when England played Australia in the second Test – and won by an innings and five runs. It was also the first Test in which a substitute fielder took a catch – Australian captain Billy Murdoch, having already batted, fielding for England (because W.G. Grace had hurt his finger) – caught fellow countryman Tup Scott.

THIS MATCH ALSO INCLUDED: The FIRST Test catch taken by a substitute fielder

THE ONLY
COUNTY MATCH ABANDONED
OVER THE DEATH
OF A NON-PLAYER

**Lancashire v Gloucestershire at Old Trafford, Manchester,
Lancashire, England. Friday 25 July 1884.**

The match between Lancashire and Gloucestershire at Old Trafford, Manchester was abandoned following the death of Martha Grace. This is the only such occurrence of a game being stopped over the death of a non-player. Martha Grace, born on 18 July 1812, was the first woman to appear in *Wisden*'s Births and Deaths of Cricketers section, listed as 'Grace, Mrs H.M. (mother of W.G., E.M. and G.F.)'. Forty-six years later, the death of Mrs W.G. Grace was recorded in *Wisden*'s obituary section.

THE FIRST
BATSMAN TO HIT
A DOUBLE CENTURY
IN A TEST MATCH

**W.L. MURDOCH, ENGLAND V AUSTRALIA AT THE OVAL, KENNINGTON,
SURREY, ENGLAND. TUESDAY 12 AUGUST 1884.**

The two teams met for the third and final Test of the 1884 rubber with England leading 1-0. Billy Murdoch, the Australian captain, batting at number three, was 145 not out at stumps on the first day and moved his score on to 211 – then the highest Test score – before he was caught by Edmund Peate off Billy Barnes's bowling. Australia made 551 off 311 four-ball overs. During Australia's innings, all 11 England players took a turn to bowl, the first time such an event occurred. England wicketkeeper, the Honourable Alfred Lyttelton, bowled two spells and Walter Read and W.G. Grace kept wicket while he took his turn with the ball. Lyttelton, who wore his pads while he bowled, amazingly, turned out to be England's most successful bowler, delivering a dozen overs, five maidens and taking four wickets for 19. It was all rather in vain, however, as the match

11 BOWLERS

The next time all 11 players bowled was on 11 March 1980 in a match between Pakistan and Australia. The first day and part of the second at the Iqbal Stadium, Faisalabad in Pakistan was washed out by rain. Australia then made 617, with captain Greg Chappell hitting 235 and Graham Yallop 172. By the time the innings came to an end there were only seven hours and 15 minutes of play left. In that time Pakistan made 382 for two and Chappell called upon all 11 players to bowl, but only Geoff Dymock took a wicket (the other wicket was a run out). Greg Chappell took a turn behind the stumps as wicketkeeper Rodney Marsh bowled ten overs, including a maiden, to end with figures of nought for 51. It was the first time in any Test involving Pakistan that both captains scored centuries (Javed Miandad was 106 not out at close of play). Pakistan wicketkeeper Taslim Arif opened his side's innings and was 210 not out, meaning he was on the pitch for the entire match.

petered out into a draw. W.G. Grace is believed to be the only player to make a dismissal off the first ball as a wicketkeeper in Tests when he caught Billy Midwinter on the leg side off Lyttelton's first lob.

THIS MATCH WAS ALSO INCLUDED: The FIRST time all 11 players in a side took a turn to bowl • The ONLY time a wicketkeeper has made a dismissal off the first ball in a Test match

THE ONLY
CRICKETER TO SCORE A CENTURY AND TAKE ALL TEN WICKETS IN AN INNINGS IN BRITAIN SINCE 1864

W.G. GRACE, MCC V OXFORD UNIVERSITY AT THE UNIVERSITY PARKS, OXFORD, ENGLAND. MONDAY 21 JUNE 1886.

Oxford University won the toss and decided to bat. They made 142 with captain Herbert Page the top scorer with 49. At close of play on the first day MCC were 83 for nought, with W.G. Grace on 50. The Grand Old Man scored 104 before he was out lbw and MCC finished on 260 all out.

Oxford University made 90 with Grace taking all ten wickets at a cost of 49 runs. Four of his victims were bowled, four caught, one stumped and one lbw. MCC won by an innings and 28 runs.

1864 is a significant date as this marks the first publication of *Wisden*, after which complete records exist (see page 47).

THE ONLY
TEST CRICKETER OF WHOM NO PHOTOGRAPH EXISTS
J. MCILWRAITH, AUSTRALIA V ENGLAND AT THE OVAL, KENNINGTON, SURREY, ENGLAND. THURSDAY 12 AUGUST 1886.

John McIlwraith, a member of the fifth Australian team to visit England, is the lost man of Test cricket. He was born at Collingwood, Melbourne, Victoria on 7 September 1857 and played just one Test, in which he scored two and (opening the second innings) seven. He is the only Test cricketer of whom there is no photograph. He died at Camberwell, Melbourne, Victoria on 5 July 1938, two months before his 81st birthday.

THE FIRST
TEST CAPTAIN TO WIN A TOSS AND ASK THE OTHER SIDE TO BAT
P.S. MCDONNELL, AUSTRALIA V ENGLAND AT SYDNEY CRICKET GROUND, MOORE PARK, MOORE PARK ROAD, SYDNEY, NEW SOUTH WALES, AUSTRALIA. FRIDAY 28 JANUARY 1887.

Australia's Percy McDonnell won the call at the Sydney Cricket Ground in the first Test against England. It seemed his strategy would pay off when he used just two bowlers – Charlie Turner six for 15 and J.J. Ferris four for 27 – to dismiss England for just 45 with only one player (George Lohmann) making double figures with 17. Australia then made 119 before England returned to the fray and hit 184, Ferris taking five for 76 and just missing by one getting ten wickets in a match. England then bowled Australia out for 97 (Billy Barnes six for 28) to win the game by 13 runs. McDonnell repeated his gamble in February 1888 with the same result – victory for England.

THE FIRST
INNINGS OF MORE THAN 800
IN FIRST CLASS CRICKET
SMOKERS V NON-SMOKERS
AT EAST MELBOURNE CRICKET GROUND, JOLIMONT, MELBOURNE, VICTORIA, AUSTRALIA. THURSDAY 17 MARCH 1887.

Non-Smokers won the toss and decided to bat in the match against the Smokers. Over the first three days the Non-Smokers scored 803 – the first innings of more than 800 in First Class cricket. Arthur Shrewsbury opened the innings and scored 236, while his partner William Bruce hit 131 as they made 196 for the first wicket. Billy Gunn scored 150 and Billy Barnes was absent hurt so the Non-Smokers lost nine wickets. The Smokers made 356, with opener Eugene Palmer hitting 113 and Billy Bates taking six for 73. The Smokers followed on and were 135 for five when the match petered out into a draw. The teams were made up of English tourists and local players. The East Melbourne Cricket Ground was demolished in 1921.

THE LAST
ALL-AMATEUR
COUNTY CHAMPIONSHIP TEAM
GLOUCESTERSHIRE V YORKSHIRE AT SPA GROUND, GLOUCESTER, GLOUCESTERSHIRE, ENGLAND. THURSDAY 30 JUNE 1887.

The last county to field an all-amateur side was Gloucestershire in the County Championship against Yorkshire. The Gloucestershire captain W.G. Grace won the toss and decided to bat. They made 369, with W.G. top scoring at 92. Yorkshire made 300 all out with E.M. Grace, who had opened the Gloucestershire innings with his brother, taking seven for 120. In the second innings W.G. Grace dropped down the order to number three and made 183 not out and the match ended in a draw. The amateur status was abolished after the end of the 1962 season.

THE ONLY

IMAGINARY TEST MATCH

AN IMAGINARY CRICKET MATCH, 1887.

At Lord's hangs a painting entitled *An Imaginary Cricket Match*, previously called *Australia v England – An Ideal Cricket Match at Lord's*. It was painted by Sir Robert Ponsonby Staples (1853–1943) and George Hamilton Barrable (*fl* 1873–1887). Sir Robert Ponsonby Staples was born at Dundee and painted portraits, genre scenes and landscapes. George Hamilton Barrable concentrated on interior and domestic subjects. The painting features a host of well-known cricketers, plus 40 public figures standing on the boundary, including the Prince and Princess of Wales (later King Edward VII and Queen Alexandra) with the Prince of Wales's mistress Lillie Langtry nearby. The painting is of an imaginary Test match at a very exciting stage in the proceedings. Below the picture of the Test match are portraits of 22 players (who in reality never played against each other in the two sides depicted). The players include W.G. Grace, F.R. Spofforth, T.W. Garrett and W.W. Read. When the painting was completed only two Tests had been staged at Lord's and the pavilion in the artwork was replaced by the present one in 1890.

THE FIRST

TEST MATCH IN WHICH BOTH OPENERS WERE OUT FOR DUCKS

AUSTRALIA V ENGLAND AT OLD TRAFFORD, MANCHESTER, LANCASHIRE, ENGLAND. FRIDAY 31 AUGUST 1888.

The 30th international between the two old enemies was, as with so many Tests in Manchester, affected by rain. The pitch was soft and wet, thanks to heavy rain beforehand, giving the team batting first – England – a big advantage. The home side made 172 all out, with opener and captain W.G. Grace leading the way with a top score of 38. At stumps on the first day Australia were 32 for two. The second day was blighted as far as Australia were concerned by a hot sun that left the pitch sticky. Eighteen wickets fell

JACK THE RIPPER?

In London on 31 August 1888 Mary Ann Nichols became the first victim of Jack the Ripper. Eight days later, on 8 September 'Dark Annie' Chapman became the Ripper's second victim. That same day, the Blackheath Club played a cricket match against the Brothers Christopherson at Blackheath in south east London. Playing for Blackheath was 31-year-old barrister and teacher Montague John Druitt who was celebrated for his great strength in his arms and wrists. In 1894 Sir Melville Macnaghten, the head of CID at Scotland Yard, named Druitt as his favoured candidate for Jack the Ripper and, indeed, several authors have written books suggesting Druitt was the Ripper but substantial evidence to confirm this allegation is lacking.

before lunch, a Test record, and at one stage in their second innings Australia were seven for six – both openers, as well as numbers three and four out without troubling the scorers – before collapsing to 70 all out to give England a victory by an innings and 21 runs.

THE LAST

ENGLISH SEASON
WITH FOUR-BALL OVERS

1888.

The number of deliveries (excluding wides and no-balls) per over is now set at six worldwide but until 1888 an over consisted of four balls. The most four-ball overs delivered in an innings was 123 by Edinburgh-born David Buchanan in a 12-a-side match between the Gentlemen of England against Cambridge University on 24 and 25 May 1880 at Fenner's. Opening the innings, Buchanan bowled 50 maidens and took five Cambridge wickets for 146. Away from the pitch, he fathered eight children. The most four-ball overs bowled in a season was 2,631.2 by Alfred Shaw in 1876 for Nottinghamshire and MCC. In 1889 the number of balls per over was increased to five.

THE ONLY
ENGLISH TEST CRICKETER TO BECOME A SUCCESSFUL HOLLYWOOD ACTOR

C.A. SMITH, ENGLAND V SOUTH AFRICA AT ST GEORGE'S PARK, PORT ELIZABETH, EASTERN CAPE, SOUTH AFRICA. TUESDAY 12 MARCH 1889.

Charles Aubrey Smith was born in the City of London, the son of a doctor, and educated at Charterhouse and Cambridge. Unlike other thespians, Smith's entry in *Who's Who* was a paradigm of modesty. It simply listed his name, profession (film actor), date of birth, the names of his parents, the year of his marriage (1896) but not the name of his wife, the fact he had one daughter, his education, his hobby (cricket), his address and his clubs.

Prior to becoming an actor Smith was a fine cricketer, winning a Blue at Cambridge in 1882. That year he joined Sussex where he played for the next 14 seasons, captaining the side from 1887 until 1889. In 1887–1888 he toured Australia, winning 14 and losing two of the 25 fixtures, and the following winter captained the first English side (Major Warton's) to venture to South Africa. The side won 13 and lost four of its 19 matches. On 12–13 March 1889 the tourists played South Africa at St George's Park, Port Elizabeth. This later became known as the first South African Test, although it wasn't recognized as such at the time, and was the first First Class match in the union. In the Test Smith scored three and took five for 19 and two for 42, playing his part in England's victory. On the tour Smith took 134 wickets at a cost of 7.61 runs apiece. He stayed in South Africa after the tour to captain Transvaal against Kimberley in the first Currie Cup match on 5, 7 and 8 April 1890.

A useful right arm fast bowler, his best bowling performances were taking five for eight for Sussex against Cambridge in 1885 and seven for 16 against the MCC at Lord's in 1890. His highest innings was 142 for Sussex against Hampshire at Hove in 1888. He stood over 6 feet (1.83 m) tall and had such a peculiar bowling action he was known as 'Round The Corner Smith'. He played 99 First Class matches for Sussex, scoring 2,315 runs averaging 14.55, and taking 208 wickets for 5,006 runs, averaging 24.06.

A sporting all-rounder, he also played outside right at football for Old Carthusians and Corinthians. Following his retirement from the sporting arena, he moved into the theatrical one, becoming an accomplished stage (making his début aged 30) and silent screen actor. In 1938 he was awarded the CBE, becoming a knight six years later.

CHARLES SMITH PLAYED IN: The FIRST Test match in South Africa • The FIRST First Class match in South Africa.
HE WAS ALSO: The ONLY player to captain England on his only Test appearance

THE ONLY
TEST CRICKETER KILLED BY A CRANE
C.A. ABSOLOM, PORT OF SPAIN, TRINIDAD. TUESDAY 30 JULY 1889.

Test cricketer Charlie Absolom died aged 43, a few days after a crane fell on him while loading the ship SS *Muriel* with sugar (some sources say bananas) at Port of Spain, Trinidad. He captured 25 wickets in four University matches but played just one Test, making 53 out of 113 in the first innings against Australia at Melbourne. In 1880, Absolom retired and nothing more was heard of him until news of his death broke nine years later.

THE FIRST
TEAM TO DECLARE
Surrey v Gloucestershire at The Oval, Kennington, Surrey, England.
Saturday 8 June 1889.

In 1889 the Laws of the game were changed to permit a captain to declare his side's innings closed if he so wanted. The first team to take advantage of this alteration were Surrey, whose captain John Shuter declared their second innings closed at 338 for seven in a county match against Gloucestershire. The opposition captain was W.G. Grace. It was obviously a good decision by Shuter as Surrey won by 250 runs.

THE FIRST
COUNTY CHAMPIONSHIP
MATCH

Gloucestershire v Yorkshire at Ashley Down Ground, Bristol, Gloucestershire, England. Monday 12 May 1890.

The first match in the County Championship was between Gloucestershire and Yorkshire. Gloucestershire won the toss and decided to bat. Captain W.G. Grace opened the innings with his brother E.M. and faced the first over (from Bobby Peel), which was a maiden. Amateur William Whitwell then bowled the second over to E.M. who was out for the first duck, caught by Lord Hawke. In the same over Octavius Radcliffe scored the first run. The home county made 194, 101 of which were scored by Jimmie Cranston – the first centurion. Yorkshire were all out for 330, which included 107 from George Ulyett, the first professional to score a century. In their second knock Gloucestershire made 178 and Yorkshire won by eight wickets after scoring 43.

THIS MATCH ALSO INCLUDED: The FIRST County Championship maiden • The FIRST County Championship wicket • The FIRST County Championship duck • The FIRST County Championship runs • The FIRST County Championship century • The FIRST century by a professional in a County Championship match

THE FIRST
TEST MATCH ABANDONED
WITHOUT A BALL BOWLED

ENGLAND V AUSTRALIA AT OLD TRAFFORD, MANCHESTER, LANCASHIRE, ENGLAND. MONDAY 25 AUGUST 1890.

England, captained by W.G. Grace, and Australia, captained by Billy Murdoch, were ready to do battle at Old Trafford in the third Test of the Ashes series but the rain came and never left. No toss was made and the match was abandoned without a ball bowled.

THE ONLY
LONDON UNDERGROUND STATION NAMED AFTER A CRICKET GROUND

**OVAL, NORTHERN LINE, LONDON BOROUGH OF LAMBETH, ENGLAND.
OPENED THURSDAY 18 DECEMBER 1890.**

The first cricket match was played at The Oval in 1845. On 22 August of that year Surrey CCC was founded at The Horns pub in Kennington and a lease was obtained for The Oval from the ground's owner, the Duchy of Cornwall. Forty-five years later, the Tube station was opened as part of the City & South London Railway. The station is now on the Morden branch of the Northern Line.

LORD'S TUBE STATION

Although Oval is now the only Tube station named for a cricket ground, that was not always the case. On 5 November 1932 the name of Gillespie Road Tube station was changed to Arsenal after lobbying from Herbert Chapman, the manager of the Gunners. The members and committee of MCC watched this with keen interest.

On 13 April 1868 the Metropolitan Railway opened St John's Wood Road station between Baker Street and Swiss Cottage. On April Fool's Day 1925 it was renamed St John's Wood. MCC began a campaign to change the name again, this time to Lord's, which they reckoned would be great publicity for the ground. The company running the Underground agreed and on 11 June 1939 the station's name was changed to Lord's.

Unfortunately, due to increased passenger numbers, the Bakerloo Line took over some of the services on the Stanmore link (now the Jubilee Line) out of Baker Street and on 20 November 1939 Lord's closed, never to reopen. The building was demolished in 1969.

THE FIRST

KING PAIR IN TEST CRICKET

W. ATTEWELL, ENGLAND V AUSTRALIA AT SYDNEY CRICKET GROUND, MOORE PARK, MOORE PARK ROAD, SYDNEY, NEW SOUTH WALES, AUSTRALIA. WEDNESDAY 3 FEBRUARY 1892.

William 'Dick' Attewell was a medium pace bowler for Nottinghamshire who made his Test debut at Adelaide on 12 December 1884. Just over seven years later he became the first batsman in Test history to bag a king pair – out first ball in both innings. To add to Attewell's personal misery, Australia won by 72 runs. It was his penultimate Test but in his last Test match he scored 43 not out, his highest score in international cricket. In the match Bobby Abel became the first Englishman to carry his bat in a Test match when he was 132 not out in the first innings. In the second innings he only made one.

THIS MATCH INCLUDED: The FIRST Englishman to carry his bat in a Test match

THE FIRST

SHEFFIELD SHIELD MATCH

NEW SOUTH WALES V SOUTH AUSTRALIA AT ADELAIDE OVAL, WAR MEMORIAL DRIVE, NORTH ADELAIDE, SOUTH AUSTRALIA, AUSTRALIA. FRIDAY 16 DECEMBER 1892.

In 1891–1892 England toured Australia under the leadership of W.G. Grace. The patron of the tour was the 3rd Earl of Sheffield and, so impressed was he by the reception given to the England team, that he donated 150 guineas (worth about £9,400 now) to help advance cricket in the colonies. The newly instituted Australian Cricket Council used the money to buy a shield measuring 3 feet 10 inches x 2 feet 6 inches (117 cm x 76 cm), that bore the coats of arms of Sheffield and Australia.

The first states to compete in the Sheffield Shield were New South Wales, South Australia and Victoria, who won the competition. The first match played in the Sheffield Shield, Australia's premier First Class competition, was a contest between South Australia (212 and 330) who beat New South Wales (337 and 148). New South Wales won the toss and elected to bat. George Giffen, the captain of South Australia, bowled the first ball in the competition to Sammy Jones. He took Jones's wicket in the same over. Giffen also took the wicket of Harry Moses, the New South Wales captain, on 99 and so the honour of the first Sheffield Shield century went to Harry Donnan who scored 120. Giffen took the first five- wicket haul in an innings of the Sheffield Shield with six for 133. He also top scored with 75 in South Australia's first innings of 212. About 15,000 spectators watched the match. Charles Bannerman, who scored the first run in Test cricket, was one of the umpires. Queensland joined the competition in 1926–1927, followed in 1947–1948 (on an experimental basis) by Western Australia and (also on an experimental basis) by Tasmania in 1977–1978.

For nine years, from 1999 until 2008, the Sheffield Shield was known as the Pura Cup, for sponsorship reasons. The state sides have all since changed their names and play as New South Wales Blues, Queensland Bulls, Southern Redbacks, Tasmanian Tigers, Victorian Bullrangers and Western Warriors.

THIS MATCH INCLUDED: The **FIRST** Sheffield Shield century
• The **FIRST** five-wicket haul in a Sheffield Shield innings

———•••———

THE FIRST
BOWLER TO TAKE
FOUR WICKETS WITH FOUR BALLS
IN THE COUNTY CHAMPIONSHIP
F.J. SHACKLOCK, NOTTINGHAMSHIRE V SOMERSET AT TRENT BRIDGE, NOTTINGHAM, NOTTINGHAMSHIRE, ENGLAND. SATURDAY 3 JUNE 1893.

———•••———

Frank Shacklock of Nottinghamshire became the first bowler to take four wickets with four balls in the County Championship when he dismissed a quartet of Somerset batsmen as he took eight for 46. Nottinghamshire won by 225 runs.

THE FIRST
BATSMAN TO SCORE
1,000 RUNS
IN TEST CRICKET

A. SHREWSBURY, ENGLAND V AUSTRALIA AT LORD'S CRICKET GROUND, ST JOHN'S WOOD ROAD, ST JOHN'S WOOD, MIDDLESEX, ENGLAND. MONDAY 17 JULY 1893.

Arthur Shrewsbury of Nottinghamshire was the first player to score 1,000 runs in Test cricket when he hit 106 in the first innings – his third and last international ton – against Australia in the first Test of the 1893 season. He scored 81 in the second knock. He retired in 1902 when he was 46. At the age of 47, while in a fit of depression, he shot himself at his sister's home in Gedling, Nottinghamshire on 19 May 1903.

THE FIRST
TEST CAPTAIN TO DECLARE

A.E. STODDART, ENGLAND V AUSTRALIA AT LORD'S CRICKET GROUND, ST JOHN'S WOOD ROAD, ST JOHN'S WOOD, MIDDLESEX, ENGLAND. WEDNESDAY 19 JULY 1893.

Andrew Stoddart captained England in place of W.G. Grace who was injured. He won the toss and elected to bat. England scored 334 and bowled Australia out for 269. On the morning of the third day of the match, with the score on 234 for eight, Stoddart became the first

JIM PHILLIPS
Standing in the match was Jim Phillips, who became the first umpire to officiate in two different countries, having stood in three Tests in his native Australia. He went on to umpire in South Africa and thus became the first official to stand in three countries.

Test captain to make a declaration. Unfortunately, he was unable to capitalize on his bravery because the rain came and play was washed out after lunch.

THE ONLY
BOWLER TO TAKE A HAT-TRICK WITH THREE STUMPINGS IN FIRST CLASS CRICKET

C.L. Townsend, Gloucestershire v Somerset at College Sports Ground, Thirlestaine Road, Cheltenham, Gloucestershire, England. Tuesday 15 August 1893.

Leg-break bowler Charlie Townsend, then just 16 years old, took a hat-trick in Somerset's second innings. All three batsmen were bowled by Townsend and stumped by wicketkeeper William Brain.

THE ONLY
BOWLER TO TAKE FOUR WICKETS IN FOUR BALLS IN NEW ZEALAND FIRST CLASS CRICKET

A. DOWNES, OTAGO V AUCKLAND AT CARISBROOK, DUNEDIN, NEW ZEALAND. TUESDAY 2 JANUARY 1894.

Off-break bowler Alexander Downes became the only cricketer to take four wickets with consecutive balls in New Zealand First Class cricket in 1894. While playing for Otago against Auckland, he dismissed captain Rowland Holle, William Stemson, John Lundon and Henry Lawson in the second innings to finish with innings figures of six for 45. He took five for 35 in the first innings for match figures of 11 for 80 but, despite his efforts, Auckland won by 13 runs.

THE FIRST

TEST SIDE IN WHICH ALL 11 PLAYERS
SCORED DOUBLE FIGURES

ENGLAND V AUSTRALIA AT MELBOURNE CRICKET GROUND, JOLIMONT,
MELBOURNE, VICTORIA, AUSTRALIA. SATURDAY 29 DECEMBER 1894.

Australia won the toss and elected to field in the second Test between Australia and England. It seemed a wise decision as they bowled England out for just 75 with only two players making double figures, one of those (Andrew Stoddart) scoring just ten. Charlie Turner took five England wickets for 32. In his only Test match Aussie fast bowler Arthur Coningham took England opener Archie MacLaren's wicket with his first ball – the first time a wicket fell to the first ball of a Test match.

Australia were then dismissed for 123 at the close of the first day's play. Tom Richardson took five for 57. England rallied in their second innings with 475 all out, to become the first Test side in which all 11 batsmen reached double figures. Stoddart led the way with a Test career-best 173; Bobby Peel on 53 was the next highest scorer and the only one to reach a half-century. They then bowled out Australia for 333 to win the match by 94 runs.

THIS MATCH INCLUDED: The FIRST time a wicket fell to the first ball of a Test match.

THE FIRST
BATSMAN TO BAG PAIRS
IN CONSECUTIVE TESTS

R. PEEL, ENGLAND V AUSTRALIA AT ADELAIDE OVAL, WAR MEMORIAL DRIVE, NORTH ADELAIDE, SOUTH AUSTRALIA,
AUSTRALIA AND AT SYDNEY CRICKET GROUND, MOORE PARK, MOORE PARK ROAD, SYDNEY, NEW SOUTH WALES,
AUSTRALIA. JANUARY 1895.

Bobby Peel (1857–1941) had his unwanted achievement in the third Test at the Adelaide Oval when he was out for nought twice (bowled and then caught and bowled) and then again in the fourth Test held at Sydney

HAWKE'S HELPING HAND

Bobby Peel was born at Churwell, Leeds on 12 February 1857. A slow left-arm bowler, he played in 20 Tests and took 101 wickets. While playing for Yorkshire against Lancashire in a County Championship game in 1897 Peel was drunk and reportedly urinated on the pitch. His captain Lord Hawke sent him off the field and Peel later recalled, 'Lord Hawke put his arm round me and helped me off the ground – and out of First Class cricket. What a gentleman!'

when he was stumped in both innings on 4 February 1895. On the first occasion Australia won by 382 runs and, on the second, Australia won by an innings and 147 runs. England's cause was not helped by the absence of Bill Lockwood whose hand had been damaged by an exploding soft-drink bottle.

THE FIRST

BOWLER TO TAKE 100 TEST WICKETS

J. BRIGGS, ENGLAND V AUSTRALIA AT SYDNEY CRICKET GROUND, MOORE PARK, MOORE PARK ROAD, SYDNEY, NEW SOUTH WALES, AUSTRALIA. FRIDAY 1 FEBRUARY 1895.

Lancashire's left arm slow bowler Johnny Briggs became the first man to take 100 wickets in Test cricket when he dismissed Australian wicketkeeper Arthur Jarvis just before tea on the first day of the fourth Test of the 1894–1895 Ashes rubber. Briggs was playing in his 25th Test. Despite Briggs's four wickets in the match, Australia made 284 and then bowled England out for 65 and 72 to win by an innings and 147 runs. In the match Andrew Stoddart became the first captain to win the toss and ask Australia to bat.

THIS MATCH INCLUDED: The FIRST England captain to win the toss and ask Australia to bat

THE FIRST
BATSMAN TO SCORE
1,000 FIRST CLASS RUNS
IN MAY

W.G. Grace, Thursday 30 May 1895.

W.G. Grace scored 169 for Gloucestershire against Middlesex at Lord's to become the first player to score 1,000 First Class runs in May – the first full month of the cricket season. He finished with 1,016, averaging 112.88, and, to add to his pleasure, Gloucestershire won by five wickets.

THE FIRST
BATSMAN TO SCORE
A FIRST CLASS
QUADRUPLE
CENTURY

A.C. MACLAREN, LANCASHIRE V SOMERSET AT COUNTY GROUND, TAUNTON, SOMERSET, ENGLAND. MONDAY 15 JULY 1895.

Lancashire captain Archie MacLaren won the toss in the County Championship match against Somerset and decided to bat and bat and bat... and bat. By the time the Lancashire innings came to a close on the second day, the scoreboard read 801 and MacLaren was responsible for 424 of those runs – the first player to score a quadruple century in First Class cricket. Remarkably, despite the mammoth score, three of the Lancashire team were out for ducks and two more made only single figures. Arthur Paul made 177 but only one other player scored more than 50. Somerset opening bowler Ted Tyler returned figures of one for 212. Somerset made 143 in their first innings and 206 in the second, for Lancashire to win by an innings and 452 runs.

THE FIRST

PLAYER TO DO
THE TEST DOUBLE –
1,000 RUNS AND 100 WICKETS

G. GIFFEN, AUSTRALIA V ENGLAND AT OLD TRAFFORD, MANCHESTER, LANCASHIRE, ENGLAND. SATURDAY 18 JULY 1896.

George Giffen, the first South Australian to represent Australia, was the first player to score 1,000 runs and take 100 wickets in Test matches. His achievement came at Old Trafford in his 30th, and penultimate, Test. Giffen was known as 'The W.G. Grace of Australia', so it was perhaps appropriate that his achievement came on Grace's 48th birthday. He finished the match having scored 80 and six and returned figures of 19-3-48-1 and 16-1-65-3.

GEORGE GIFFEN WAS ALSO: The FIRST South Australian to represent Australia

THE ONLY

BATSMAN TO SCORE
TWO FIRST CLASS HUNDREDS
ON THE SAME DAY

K.S. Ranjitsinhji, Sussex v Yorkshire at County Ground, Eaton Road, Hove, West Sussex, England. Saturday 22 August 1896.

In 1896 Kumar Shri Ranjitsinhji became the only batsman to score two First Class centuries on the same day. Resuming his innings on nought not out, he hit exactly 100 for Sussex against Yorkshire at County Ground, Hove. In fact, Ranji made 52 per cent of his county's runs, as they were all out for 191 and forced to follow on. He was on 125 not out when the match petered out into a draw.

THE FIRST
PLAYER TO BE THE SOLITARY
WISDEN CRICKETER OF THE YEAR
W.G. GRACE, 1896.

The first time a single figure was chosen as *Wisden*'s Cricketer of the Year was in 1896, when the Grand Old Man of cricket W.G. Grace was chosen.

THE FIRST
COUNTY CHAMPIONSHIP
SIDE TO GO A
SEASON WITHOUT A WIN
DERBYSHIRE. 1897.

In 1897 Derbyshire played 16 games in the County Championship, drawing seven and losing nine. Unsurprisingly, they finished bottom of the 14-county table, although the system determining who finished where was utterly bizarre. Teams got one point for a win, lost a point for a defeat and got nothing for a draw. The counties did not even each play the same number of games. County champions Lancashire and runners-up Surrey played 26 while third-placed Essex played just 16. The position of teams in the table was decided by the percentage of finished matches. Lancashire won 16 of their 26 games to gain 16 points but lost three games, so were deducted three points to finish on 13. Surrey won 17 of their 26 games to gain 17 points but lost four games so were deducted four points to also finish on 13.

However, because drawn games were adjudged not to have been finished, the authorities divided the games with a result (win/lose) by the total number of games played, which gave the championship to Lancashire, who had finished 68.42 per cent of their games compared to Surrey's 61.90. Poor old Derbyshire, as well as not winning a game, were adjudged to have finished minus 100 per cent of their games.

THE FIRST
LEFT-HANDED BATSMAN TO
SCORE A TEST CENTURY

J. DARLING, AUSTRALIA V ENGLAND AT SYDNEY CRICKET GROUND, MOORE PARK, MOORE PARK
ROAD, SYDNEY, NEW SOUTH WALES, AUSTRALIA. THURSDAY 16 DECEMBER 1897.

In the first Test of the 1897–1898 Ashes series England were captained by Archie MacLaren, replacing Andrew Stoddart whose mother had died. England won the toss and elected to bat, making 551, with MacLaren leading from the front with 109 and Ranji scoring 175. Aussie Jim Kelly became the first wicketkeeper to prevent any byes in a total exceeding 500. Australia in reply were bowled out for 237 with John Hearne taking five for 42. MacLaren enforced the follow-on and Joe Darling became the first left-hander to score a Test century. He was finally out for 101. Clem Hill made 96, as the Aussies made 408 with Hearne taking four for 99. England reached Australia's total, scoring 96 for the loss of one wicket to win comprehensively.

THIS MATCH ALSO INCLUDED: The FIRST wicketkeeper to prevent any byes in a total exceeding 500

THE FIRST
BOWLER TO BE NO-BALLED
FOR THROWING IN A TEST

E. JONES, AUSTRALIA V ENGLAND AT MELBOURNE CRICKET GROUND,
JOLIMONT, MELBOURNE, VICTORIA, AUSTRALIA. TUESDAY 4 JANUARY
1898.

In 1896 Ernie Jones, a short but compact fast bowler, toured England and *Wisden* referred to 'his pace of an express train with a bent arm'. It would not be the last time that his bowling action was called into question. In the second Test of the 1897–1898 Ashes series, umpire Jim Phillips, standing in his 15th Test, called Jones for throwing. Jones reconsidered his run-up and length and escaped any further censures. *Wisden* sources vary as to whether Jones was called once or twice in the match. *The Wisden Book Of Test Cricket* (Frindall) says that Jones was called once but *Wisden On The Ashes* (Lynch), based on the original almanack reports, claims that he was no-balled twice.

—◆•◆—

THE LAST
TEST APPEARANCE BY
W.G. GRACE

W.G. GRACE, ENGLAND V AUSTRALIA AT TRENT BRIDGE, NOTTINGHAM, NOTTINGHAMSHIRE, ENGLAND. SATURDAY 3 JUNE 1899.

England and Australia drew the first match of the first five-Test series. It was also the first Test played at Trent Bridge, Nottingham and was also W.G. Grace's last match as captain and last match for England. At 50 years and 320 days old when it ended, he was the oldest Test captain. He was not the oldest Test player – that honour would go to Wilf Rhodes who, ironically, was making his Test debut in the match (see 1930, page 116).

THIS MATCH ALSO INCLUDED: The FIRST player over 50 to appear in a Test match • The FIRST Test match staged at Trent Bridge

—◆•◆—

THE FIRST
TEST MATCH STAGED
AT HEADINGLEY

ENGLAND V AUSTRALIA AT HEADINGLEY, St MICHAEL'S LANE, LEEDS, YORKSHIRE, ENGLAND. THURSDAY 29 JUNE 1899.

Headingley played host to a Test match for the first time when England met Australia in the third Test. England bowler Johnny Briggs suffered an epileptic seizure on the first day, was confined to Cheadle Asylum and missed the rest of the season. The match ended as a draw when the rain came.

THE ONLY
BATSMAN TO HIT
A BALL OVER THE
CURRENT LORD'S PAVILION

A.E. TROTT, MCC V AUSTRALIANS AT LORD'S CRICKET GROUND, ST JOHN'S WOOD ROAD, ST JOHN'S WOOD, MIDDLESEX, ENGLAND. MONDAY 31 JULY 1899.

Australian Albert Trott, playing for the MCC against the touring Australians, became the only batsman to hit a ball over the current Lord's pavilion, smashing Monty Noble out of the ground on his way to 41. Despite his best efforts – he also took three wickets – the Australians won by nine wickets.

THE LAST
ENGLISH SEASON WITH
FIVE-BALL OVERS

1899.

In 1889 the number of deliveries per over was increased to five from four. The change lasted 11 seasons before the number was again increased, this time to six, in 1900, and it has stayed that way apart from one experimental season. The most five-ball overs delivered in an innings was 100.1 by Alfred Shaw for Sussex against Nottinghamshire at Trent Bridge on 16 and 17 May 1895. Notts scored a mammoth 726 all out and Shaw took four for 168. The remainder of the bowling was divided between six other players and Shaw's nearest rival bowled just 38 overs. Unsurprisingly, Nottinghamshire won by an innings and 378 runs. The next year John Hearne bowled the most five-ball overs in a season – 2,003.1 for Middlesex.

THE FIRST
BATSMAN TO SCORE
3,000 FIRST CLASS RUNS IN A SEASON

K.S. Ranjitsinhji, 1899.

The first Indian to play Test cricket, Ranji was also the first player to score 3,000 runs in a First Class season. Playing for Sussex in 1899 (also the first year that he was captain), in 34 games he hit 3,159 runs with a highest score of 197 and an average of 63.18. He hit just eight centuries and 17 half-centuries. To prove it was no fluke, Ranji, who wore immaculate silk shirts on the field, repeated the accomplishment in 1900, although this time he scored 3,065 runs from just 26 games. His highest score was 275 and he averaged 87.57. He hit 11 centuries and ten fifties. Cricket historians credit him with, if not inventing, then certainly popularizing the leg glance. He scored 24,692 First Class runs. Oddly, before he arrived in England, he had never played a proper game of cricket. He suffered from hay fever and detested England's cold, wet winters. In 1912 at the Scarborough Festival he wore several layers to keep warm. *The Times* reported, 'Had the cold lasted, he certainly would not have been able to pass out of the dressing room door.'

THE FIRST
VICTIM OF A GOOGLY

S. COE, LEICESTERSHIRE V MIDDLESEX AT LORD'S CRICKET GROUND, ST JOHN'S WOOD ROAD, ST JOHN'S WOOD, MIDDLESEX, ENGLAND. THURSDAY 20 JULY 1900.

Basically, a googly is an off-break bowled with a leg-break action. The googly was invented by B.J.T. Bosanquet – hence its name Bosie in Australia – in 1897 while he was playing the game Twisti Twosti, in which a tennis ball was spun in different directions. After practising endlessly, Bosanquet unveiled his new action at Lords in July 1900 in the second innings of the County Championship match between Middlesex and Leicestershire. Leicestershire won the toss and decided to bat. They were dismissed for 184. Middlesex scored 224 with Bosanquet hitting 136 in 110 minutes. Leicestershire hit 342 in their second innings and Bosanquet took his first wicket with a googly. Samuel Coe was on 98 when he faced Bosanquet – the ball bounced four times before Coe missed it and he was stumped by wicketkeeper William Robertson.

THE ONLY
BATSMAN TO SCORE A FIRST CLASS HUNDRED
IN BOTH INNINGS BEFORE LUNCH
G.L. Jessop, Gloucestershire v Yorkshire at Park Avenue Cricket Ground, Horton Park Avenue, Bradford, West Yorkshire, England. Monday 24 July 1900.

Gilbert Jessop scored 104 before lunch on the second day of the match. On the third day he scored 139 including seven sixes off Wilfred Rhodes. In the first innings Lord Hawke caught him off the bowling of Rhodes and in the second innings he was caught by John Tunnicliffe, again off Rhodes. Jessop was a prolific scorer of fast hundreds. Between 1897 and 1913 he hit 11 centuries in an hour or less.

THE ONLY
TIME CRICKET WAS
PLAYED AT THE OLYMPICS
PARIS, FRANCE. MONDAY 20 AUGUST 1900.

Great Britain won the only Olympic gold medal for cricket when they beat France at the Exhibition Ground, Vincennes. Each side fielded 12 players and Great Britain batted first. They were all out for 117, Frederick Cuming of the MCC topping the scores with 38. Captain Charles Beachcroft was second with 23. For France W. Andersen took four wickets. In reply France were bowled out for 78 with Frederick W. Christian taking seven Gallic wickets. In their second innings the British side scored 145 for five declared before dismissing the French for just 26 with only five minutes to spare before end of play. Great Britain won by 158 runs. Montagu Toller took a remarkable seven for nine.

The Devon County Wanderers Club represented Britain while France was represented by the French Athletic Club Union (which consisted almost entirely of Englishmen living in France and playing for the then champions of France, the Albion Cricket Club, or for the Standard Athletic Club).

THE FIRST
BATSMAN OUT FOR 99 IN A TEST MATCH
C. HILL, AUSTRALIA V ENGLAND AT MELBOURNE CRICKET GROUND, JOLIMONT, MELBOURNE, VICTORIA, AUSTRALIA. THURSDAY 2 JANUARY 1902

Australia's Clem Hill became the first batsman out for 99 in a Test match when Arthur Jones caught him off Sydney Barnes's bowling on the second day of the second Test against England at Melbourne Cricket Ground. The 99 was the Aussie team's second highest score in a total of 353 as Australia won by 229 runs. In the third Test, at the Adelaide Oval, Hill was out for 98 in the first innings and was bowled for 97 in the second to become the only player out in the 90s in three successive Test matches.

CLEM HILL WAS ALSO: The ONLY batsman out in the 90s in three successive Test innings

THE FIRST
TEST MATCH STAGED AT EDGBASTON
ENGLAND V AUSTRALIA AT EDGBASTON, EDGBASTON ROAD, BIRMINGHAM, WARWICKSHIRE, ENGLAND. THURSDAY 29 MAY 1902.

Edgbaston hosted its first Test match when England played Australia in the first game of the 1902 rubber. England, captained by Archie MacLaren and featuring C.B. Fry, Ranjitsinhji, the Honourable Stanley Jackson, Johnny Tyldesley, Dick Lilley, Gilbert Jessop and Wilf Rhodes, made 376. Australia were then bowled out for just 36 with only opener Victor Trumper, with 18, scoring in double figures and Rhodes taking seven for 17. Enforcing the follow-on, the rain stopped England winning the match and Australia were 46 for two when the match ended.

THE FIRST
CAPTAIN OUT FOR A PAIR IN A TEST

J. DARLING, AUSTRALIA V ENGLAND AT BRAMALL LANE, SHEFFIELD, SOUTH YORKSHIRE, ENGLAND. FRIDAY 4 JULY 1902.

25 years after the first Test match Joe Darling (1870–1946) became the first captain to be out for a pair. He led a strong Australian side in England, winning the Test series by two to one during a wet, cold summer. The Aussies lost two matches on the tour. It was during the third Test, which Australia won by 143 runs, that Darling achieved his unwanted feat. In the first innings, batting at number four, he was out first ball caught by Len Braund off the bowling of Sydney Barnes. In the second Darling coincidentally fell to the same pair – caught Braund bowled Barnes.

JOE DARLING

Edinburgh-born John Darling (1831–1905) did not approve of his son's sporting activities and, when Joe was 15, he was sent to an agricultural college. Joe later worked in a bank and managed one of the family wheat farms but the lure of the willow was too much and in 1893 he began playing inter-colonial cricket. That year on 3 May he married Alice Francis and went on to father ten sons and five daughters. In 1894 Joe Darling made his Test debut. Six years later, he retired to manage a remote 10,000-acre (4,047-hectare) sheep station in Tasmania, bought for him by his father who threatened to disinherit Joe unless he took charge of it. Joe Darling did not play cricket again until December 1901 when he captained Australia in the first three Tests against Archie MacLaren's English tourists. He retired from Test cricket in 1905 (the year his father died) and from First Class cricket in 1907–1908. He was an outspoken critic of the Australian Board of Control for International Cricket Matches (now known as Cricket Australia), calling its members 'dead heads'. He later became a successful wool seller and politician in the Tasmanian Legislative Council in 1921 and held his seat until his death on 2 January 1946 after surgery for a ruptured gall bladder.

THE FIRST

BATSMAN TO SCORE A CENTURY IN A TEST MATCH BEFORE LUNCH

V.T. TRUMPER, AUSTRALIA v ENGLAND

AT OLD TRAFFORD, MANCHESTER, LANCASHIRE, ENGLAND. THURSDAY 24 JULY 1902.

Victor Trumper became the first batsman to hit a ton before lunch in a Test match when he hit 103 in the fourth Test of the 1902 series. He was able to add only one more run to his total after lunch before Dick Lilley caught him off the bowling of Wilfred Rhodes. Australia won the match by three runs.

THE FIRST

NUMBER 11 BATSMAN TO SCORE A CENTURY IN FIRST CLASS AUSTRALIAN CRICKET

T. HASTINGS, VICTORIA v SOUTH AUSTRALIA AT MELBOURNE CRICKET GROUND, JOLIMONT, MELBOURNE, VICTORIA, AUSTRALIA. FRIDAY 2 JANUARY 1903.

Wicketkeeper Thomas Hastings was the first number 11 batsman to hit a ton in First Class Australian cricket. Batting for Victoria against South Australia at Melbourne Cricket Ground, he came in when the score was 261 for nine. With Matthew Ellis he took the score to 472 and he remained undefeated on 106. Victoria won by 179 runs. In a career spread over 22 years, Hastings played only 15 First Class matches and, unsurprisingly, 106 was his highest score. He averaged 11.95. Hastings died on 19 June 1938 at North Brighton, Victoria, Adelaide. He was 73.

THE FIRST
BATSMAN TO SCORE 2,000
RUNS IN TEST CRICKET

C. Hill, Australia v England at Adelaide Oval, War Memorial Drive, North Adelaide, South Australia, Australia. Friday 15 January 1904.

Australian left-hander Clem Hill became the first batsman to score 2,000 runs in Test cricket. He achieved the feat on his home ground, the Adelaide Oval, against the old enemy, England. He was also the first player to score 3,000 runs in Test cricket. He achieved the feat on the same ground seven years later, on 12 January 1911, when he was captaining Australia in the third Test, which South Africa won by 38 runs.

CLEM HILL WAS ALSO: The FIRST player to score 3,000 runs in Test cricket

---

THE LAST
SURVIVOR OF THE FIRST
OXFORD-CAMBRIDGE MATCH
SIR HERBERT JENNER-FUST, SATURDAY 30 JULY 1904.

Sir Herbert Jenner-Fust, who died aged 98 at Hill Court, Falfield, Gloucestershire in the summer of 1904, was the last survivor of the first Oxford-Cambridge match in 1827. He scored 47 out of Cambridge's 92 in the rain-ruined game. An Old Etonian and president of the MCC, Jenner as he was known in his playing days, was an opening batsman, wicketkeeper ('pads were not heard of in my days and the player would be laughed at who attempted to protect his shins') and semi-underarm bowler, and was described by Lord Harris as 'the first gentleman player in the country'. Jenner retired from competitive cricket to practise law. Despite the fact that Jenner's son played alongside W.G. Grace, Jenner 'never took the trouble to see W.G. Grace play'. Jenner's son, also Herbert, died on 11 November 1940, aged 99. Together, they spanned an era of 134 years, eight months and 20 days.

THE FIRST
PLAYER TO SCORE
TWO CENTURIES
AND TAKE TEN WICKETS
IN A FIRST CLASS MATCH
B.J.T. BOSANQUET, MIDDLESEX V SUSSEX

AT LORD'S CRICKET GROUND, ST JOHN'S WOOD ROAD, ST JOHN'S WOOD, MIDDLESEX, ENGLAND. SATURDAY 27 MAY 1905.

The inventor of the googly (see 1900, page 88), Bernard James Tindal Bosanquet was born at home at Bulls Cross, Enfield, Middlesex, on 13 October 1877. He was educated at Eton (1891–1896), where he scored a century against Harrow at Lord's, and then Oriel College, Oxford (1897–1900), which he left without taking a degree. He represented Oxford at billiards in 1898 and 1900 and at hammer-throwing in 1899 and 1900.

He made 123 First Class appearances for Middlesex as an amateur between 1898 and 1919, taking 629 wickets. He played in six Tests and his best performance was eight for 107 against Australia at Nottingham in 1905, the year he was one of *Wisden*'s five Cricketers of the Year. Playing for Middlesex against Sussex at Lord's that year, Bosanquet became the first player to score two centuries and take ten wickets in a First Class match. In the first innings he scored 103 and was 100 not out in the second. With the ball he took three for 75 and eight for 53 as Middlesex won by 324 runs. Bosanquet died at his home, Wykehurst Farm, Coneyhurst Lane, Ewhurst, Surrey on 12 October 1936.

REGINALD BOSANQUET

Bernard Bosanquet married in 1924 at the age of 47. He had one child, a son he named Reginald Tindal Kennedy Bosanquet, who was born in 1932. Reginald went on to become a well-known television newsreader who claimed that he wore a toupee for medical reasons. He died in 1984 of pancreatic cancer.

TEST WIN BY SOUTH AFRICA

SOUTH AFRICA V ENGLAND AT OLD WANDERERS, JOHANNESBURG, GAUTENG, SOUTH AFRICA. THURSDAY 4 JANUARY 1906.

South Africa won a Test for the first time when they beat England at Old Wanderers, Johannesburg by one wicket in the first of a five-Test rubber. England won the toss and decided to bat. They made 184 and Jack Crawford scored the most runs with 44. England looked to be in pole position to win the match when they dismissed the Springboks for just 91 with only three South Africans making double figures and Walter Lees taking five for 34. England made 190 in their second innings with 51 coming from captain Plum Warner. Set a target of 284, South Africa were 134 for six at one stage. Their eventual victory was thanks to a fine 81 from Gordon White, who stayed at the crease for 265 balls over 250 minutes. It was finally Dave Nourse, with an unbeaten 93, who led the South Africans to 287 for nine and the narrowest of victories.

THE ONLY

BATSMAN TO SCORE CENTURIES
IN EACH INNINGS IN SUCCESSIVE FIRST CLASS MATCHES

T.W. HAYWARD, SURREY, ENGLAND. 4 JUNE 1906.

In the summer of 1906 opener Tom Hayward of Surrey carried his bat for 144 and hit 100 against Nottinghamshire at Trent Bridge as Surrey won by five wickets in a match that began on 4 June and ended on 6 June. The next day, he scored 143 versus Leicestershire at Aylestone Road, Leicester and 125 in the second innings. Surrey won by 110 runs. That season was a good one for him. Hayward completed 2,000 runs on 5 July and 3,000 runs on 20 August – the earliest time in any English cricket season that either milestone has been achieved. Hayward played 35 Tests for England with a top score of 137. He received his Surrey cap in 1894. He played 712 First Class matches, scoring 43,547 runs with a top score of 315 not out.

BOWLER TO TAKE TWO HAT-TRICKS IN THE SAME INNINGS IN A FIRST CLASS MATCH IN ENGLAND

A.E. Trott, Middlesex v Somerset at Lord's Cricket Ground, St John's Wood Road, St John's Wood, Middlesex, England. Wednesday 22 May 1907.

The game was Albert Trott's benefit match for Middlesex against Somerset and he went even better than two hat-tricks, taking four wickets with four balls to dismiss Talbot Lewis, Massey Poyntz, Sammy Woods and Ernie Robson (the first lbw, the others all bowled). With his next delivery Trott dislodged the bail but in those days the rules stated that the bail must be removed for a wicket to be awarded. Later in the same innings he took the wickets of Osbert Mordaunt, wicketkeeper Archie Wickham and Albert Bailey (consecutively caught, bowled and caught). He also took two catches in the innings. Trott finished the innings with figures of 8-2-20-7. Middlesex won by 166 runs but Trott was said to have been seen punching himself in the head for finishing his benefit match early. To commemorate the event Sammy Woods gave Trott a straw hat with a handpainted band showing seven rabbits running into the pavilion.

MAN TO CAPTAIN ENGLAND AT FOOTBALL AND CRICKET

R.E. FOSTER, ENGLAND V WALES AT THE RACECOURSE, MOLD ROAD, WREXHAM, CLWYD, WALES. MONDAY 3 MARCH 1902; ENGLAND V SOUTH AFRICA AT LORD'S CRICKET GROUND, ST JOHN'S WOOD ROAD, ST JOHN'S WOOD, MIDDLESEX, ENGLAND. MONDAY 1 JULY 1907.

Reginald Erskine 'Tip' Foster played football for Corinthians and made his international debut against Wales on 26 March 1900. The following year, he was named as one of *Wisden*'s Cricketers of the Year. He made his Test debut against Australia at Sydney in 1903–1904 and scored 287, the highest number of runs by a debutant. He assumed the captaincy of England at cricket in 1907 for the rubber against South Africa, but was unable to lead the winter tour to Australia because of business commitments. He played five times for England at football, scoring twice in his second game against Ireland at the Dell. He was captain for the last against Wales on 3 March 1902, a game that ended in a goalless draw before a crowd of 10,000. He played eight Tests for England. He died of diabetes on 13 May 1914, aged just 36, reputedly while 'attempting to eat a boiled egg'.

THE LAST
FIRST CLASS APPEARANCE
BY W.G. GRACE

W.G. GRACE, GENTLEMEN OF ENGLAND V SURREY WANDERERS AT THE OVAL, KENNINGTON, SURREY, ENGLAND. MONDAY 20 APRIL 1908.

W.G. Grace began his 870th and last First Class match captaining Gentlemen of England against Surrey at The Oval. It was not a great success for Grace's team as Surrey won by an innings and 41 runs. Grace opened the batting in both innings and scored 15 and 25. He bowled two overs at a cost of five runs. It was little short of three months before his 60th birthday. In 1,478 innings he had scored 54,211 runs at an average of 39.45 with a top score of 344.

THE FIRST
PLAYER TO SCORE A CENTURY
IN BOTH INNINGS OF A TEST MATCH

W. Bardsley, Australia v England at The Oval, Kennington, Surrey, England. Wednesday 11 August 1909.

Warren Bardsley became the first cricketer to score a century in both innings of a Test match when he hit 130 in the second knock of the fifth Test at The Oval. Opening the batting, he had scored 136 in the first innings. Bardsley was one of Australia's greatest left-handed batsmen. He scored 29 centuries in England and, by the time of his death in 1971, only Sir Donald Bradman and Lindsay Hassett had beaten his record of 53 centuries.

THE ONLY

BATSMAN TO CARRY HIS BAT IN BOTH INNINGS
OF A FIRST CLASS MATCH AND SCORE CENTURIES EACH TIME

C.J.B. Wood, Leicestershire v Yorkshire at Park Avenue, Bradford, Yorkshire, England. June 1911.

Cecil Wood opened the innings for Leicestershire against Yorkshire and scored 107 not out as his team reached 309. In the second knock he scored 117 not out of a total of 296. He was at the crease for eight hours and 40 minutes and did not give a chance in either innings.

THE ONLY

ENGLAND TEST CAPTAIN TO WIN OLYMPIC BOXING GOLD MEDAL

J.W.H.T. DOUGLAS, MIDDLEWEIGHT OLYMPIC FINAL, LONDON, ENGLAND. TUESDAY 27 OCTOBER 1908; ENGLAND V AUSTRALIA AT SYDNEY CRICKET GROUND, MOORE PARK, MOORE PARK ROAD, SYDNEY, NEW SOUTH WALES, AUSTRALIA. FRIDAY 15 DECEMBER 1911.

Johnny Douglas was born on 3 September 1882 at 2 Stamford Terrace, Stamford Hill, Middlesex. His debut did not augur well. His first game for Essex was against Yorkshire at the County Ground, Leyton on 15 August 1901, just a few weeks after leaving Felsted School, and he was out for a pair as Essex collapsed to 30 all out and 41 all out. Yorkshire won by an innings and 33 runs. Douglas did not bowl or take any catches. He was also out for a duck in his third innings for the county (against Gloucestershire) although he scored his first First Class runs (eight) in the second innings. Douglas played 651 First Class matches scoring 24,531 runs, including 26 hundreds, with a top score of 210 not out. He took 1,893 wickets and his best bowling performance was nine for 47.

He won a gold medal at the 1908 London Games as a middleweight boxer, beating the great Australian athlete Reginald 'Snowy' Baker. The medals were presented by Douglas's father, Johnny H. Douglas, who was president of the Amateur Boxing Association. A few days after the Olympic final, the two men had a rematch and Baker knocked Douglas out. Douglas resumed his cricketing career for Essex and became club captain in 1911, a position he held until 1928.

In the winter of the year of 1911 Douglas was selected to tour Australia. When Plum Warner became ill, Douglas took over the captaincy in his debut Test. He opened the bowling for England and took one for 62 in the first innings and four for 50 in the second, scoring a duck in his first knock and hitting 32 in the second. Under his captaincy England regained the Ashes winning the series 4-1. He was to play 23 times for England and was captain on 18 occasions (winning eight, losing eight and drawing two). Thanks to his initials, he was nicknamed 'Johnny Won't Hit Today' by Australian hecklers because of his defensive batting, but his top score in Tests was 119. He played for the amateur football sides, Corinthians and Casuals, and played for England in an Amateur Football Alliance international.

On 19 December 1930 Douglas and his father were sailing on the *Oberon* when the ship collided with another steamer, *Arcturus*, in thick fog 7 miles (11 km) south of the Laeso Trindel Lightship, Denmark. The captains of the vessels were brothers who had sent Christmas greetings to each other, unaware of just how close the boats were. The Douglases were among 42 people who perished in the disaster; it was reported that Johnny Douglas died trying to save his father.

THE ONLY
BOWLER TO TAKE
TWO HAT-TRICKS IN THE
SAME TEST MATCH

T.J. MATTHEWS, AUSTRALIA V SOUTH AFRICA AT OLD TRAFFORD, MANCHESTER, ENGLAND. TUESDAY 28 MAY 1912.

In the summer of 1912 Australia, England and South Africa met in a triangular Test tournament. The competition was not a success due to a terribly wet summer and a lack of public interest, caused by what was seen as a surfeit of cricket – nine Tests. The first match was between the Aussies and Springboks at Manchester. Australia won the toss and decided to bat.

They made 448 on the first day, with centuries from Warren Bardsley (121) and Charles Kelleway (114). Sid Pegler took 6 for 105 and South Africa were 16 for one at stumps. The next day South Africa were bowled out for 265,122 of those runs coming from Aubrey Faulkner. Bill Whitty took five for 55 and right-arm leg-break bowler Jimmy Matthews took a hat-trick, capturing the wickets of Beaumont, Pegler and Ward.

South Africa followed on and this time were dismissed for just 95 – only three players made double figures. Charles Kelleway picked up five for 33 and Matthews again took a hat-trick with the wickets of Taylor, Schwarz and Ward. The six wickets that made up his two hat-tricks were the only ones that Matthews took in the match. In each innings his final victim was South Africa's debutant wicketkeeper Tommy Ward, the only instance of a debut king pair in Test cricket. Australia won by an innings and 88 runs.

As well as his unfortunate start to Test cricket Tommy Ward had an unfortunate end to his life. On 16 February 1936 he was electrocuted, aged 48, while working at the West Springs Gold Mine.

THIS MATCH INCLUDED: The ONLY instance of a debut king pair in Test cricket

THE FIRST
ARMY AND NAVY
MATCH

ARMY V ROYAL NAVY AT LORD'S CRICKET GROUND, ST JOHN'S WOOD ROAD, ST JOHN'S WOOD, MIDDLESEX, ENGLAND. THURSDAY 30 MAY 1912.

The first First Class match between representative sides of the Army and Royal Navy took place at the home of cricket in the spring of 1912. Army won the toss and decided to bat. They made 154 with sailor Arthur Skey taking five for 27 in his only First Class appearance. The Royal Navy were bowled out for 134 and Francis Wyatt took six for 56. In their second innings the Army scored 375 with Trevor Spring scoring a career-best 117. Hugh Orr took seven for 74, which were also his career-best figures. The Army then dismissed the Royal Navy for 234 (Cecil Abercrombie, 100) to win by 161 runs. The matches lost their First Class status in 1939.

THE FIRST
TEST IN WHICH EXTRAS TOP SCORED

ENGLAND V SOUTH AFRICA AT LORD'S CRICKET GROUND, ST JOHN'S WOOD
ROAD, ST JOHN'S WOOD, MIDDLESEX, ENGLAND. MONDAY 10 JUNE 1912.

For the first time in a Test match innings, the top 'scorer' was Extras. The
Springboks won the toss and decided to put England, captained by C.B. Fry,
into the field. It was a blunder as the home team dismissed South Africa for
just 58. Only Dave Nourse reached double figures (13) but Extras top scored
with 12 byes, three leg byes and two no-balls. It took Frank Foster and Sydney
Barnes 26.1 overs to dismiss the tourists, taking five wickets apiece for 16 and
25 runs respectively. England made 337 with 119 from Reggie Spooner. Sid
Pegler took seven England wickets for 65 runs. The Springboks made 217
in their second innings but England still won, by an innings and 62 runs.

THE ONLY
WISDEN CRICKETER
OF THE YEAR NEVER TO
PLAY FIRST CLASS CRICKET
H.L. Calder, 1918.

In 1916 and 1917 the awards for *Wisden*'s Cricketers of the Year were
suspended owing to the First World War. The accolades resumed in 1918
and in both 1918 and 1919 they were presented to public school cricketers.
One of the honourees was Harry Calder, who attended Cranleigh School
and was named as one of the School Bowlers of the Year. Calder may have
been a talented schoolboy cricketer but he is the only *Wisden* Cricketer of
the Year never to play First Class cricket. He played one match for Surrey
Second XI against Minor Counties on 28–29 June 1920 and scored
nought and eight not out. With the ball, he bowled four overs for 21 and
no wickets. He died at Cape Town on 15 September 1995, 77 years after
his nomination. This is the longest period anyone has lived after being
included in *Wisden*'s list. He did not learn of his inclusion until 1994.

THE FIRST

FIRST CLASS BATSMAN
TIMED OUT

**H.J. HEYGATE, SUSSEX V SOMERSET AT COUNTY GROUND, TAUNTON,
SOMERSET, ENGLAND. THURSDAY 22 MAY 1919.**

Six months after the end of the First World War, Sussex travelled to Taunton to play Somerset in the County Championship. The match was close – Somerset made 243 in their first innings while Sussex responded with 242. In their second innings Somerset made 103 and Sussex were on 104 when their ninth wicket fell.

Number 11 was Harold Heygate who had been out for a duck in the first innings and, being crippled with rheumatism worsened by his time in the Great War trenches, had not expected to bat. He made his way slowly on to the pitch wearing his street clothes. The Somerset players appealed that he was taking too long (the Law then stated that the batsman had two minutes, rather than the current three minutes, to reach the crease) and umpire Alfred Street agreed and gave Heygate out timed out. The match ended in a tie.

Sussex appealed but the umpire's decision was upheld by the MCC, although they added that his innings should be marked as 'absent hurt' rather than out. *Wisden* reported, 'Whether or not Heygate would have crawled to the wicket, it was very unsportsmanlike that such a point should have been raised when there remained ample time to finish the match.'

THE ONLY

ENGLAND TEST CRICKETER
OFFERED A THRONE – POSSIBLY
C.B. FRY, ALBANIA. 1920.

Captain of the England Test cricket team, holder of the world long-jump record, England international footballer, rugby player for the Barbarians – C.B. Fry was probably the greatest sportsman that England has ever produced. He was also a journalist, author and politician. Charles Burgess

Fry was born on 25 April 1872 at Croydon, Surrey. He won a scholarship to Wadham College, Oxford where he continued a sporting career that had begun at Hornbrook House Preparatory School in Blackheath, south east London, where he was captain of both the cricket and football teams.

Fry worked as an assistant to his friend Ranjitsinhji at the League of Nations at Geneva in 1920. It was here that Fry – who had a reputation for telling tall stories – claimed that he was offered the throne of Albania. Fry, as he told it, was approached by an Albanian bishop who suggested that if someone could be found who would spend £10,000 a year in Albania they could have the throne. Sadly for Fry, the money proved a stumbling block and he had to turn down the offer.

He turned his mind to the House of Commons and stood three times in the Liberal interest – at the General Elections of 1922 and 1923, and at the Oxford by-election in 1924 – but lost each time. In the late 1920s and early 1930s Fry was stricken with a mental collapse. He published an autobiography, *Life Worth Living*, in 1939 in which he expressed enthusiasm for Nazi Germany and Adolf Hitler. He suggested to the Germans that they should take up cricket but Hitler and his cohorts had other, more pressing, plans. Fry died at the Middlesex Hospital, London of kidney failure on 7 September 1956. He was 84.

THE FIRST
COUNTRY TO WIN
ALL FIVE
TESTS IN A SERIES
AUSTRALIA. 1920–1921.

The first Test series after the First World War was between Warwick Armstrong's Australia and England, captained by Johnny Douglas. There were 11 debutants in the first Test at Sydney, which Australia won by 377 runs. The second Test, played at Melbourne on New Year's Eve and continuing on New Year's Day, saw Australia win by an innings and 91 runs. Australia won the third Test at the Adelaide Oval by 119 runs. The fourth Test returned to Melbourne and Australia won by eight wickets. The fifth, and final, Test was played again at Sydney and on that occasion Australia won by nine wickets.

THE ONLY
FIRST CLASS CRICKETER GIVEN OUT
'ABSENT, THOUGHT LOST ON THE TUBE'

T. Sidwell, Leicestershire v Surrey at The Oval, Kennington, Surrey, England. Friday 26 August 1921.

In the County Championship tie between Surrey and Leicestershire the away team wicketkeeper Tom Sidwell was on one not out when stumps were pulled. The next morning, he decided to make his own way to Kennington from the team hotel rather than travel with the rest of his team-mates. The result was that he became lost and had not arrived when the match began. He was listed as 'retired out' and he was not allowed to continue his innings.

THE ONLY
FATHER AND SON TO FIELD
AGAINST FATHER AND SON

W.G. QUAIFE AND B.W. QUAIFE OF WARWICKSHIRE V W. BESTWICK AND R.S. BESTWICK OF DERBYSHIRE AT COUNTY GROUND, NOTTINGHAM ROAD, DERBY, DERBYSHIRE, ENGLAND. MONDAY 5 JUNE 1922.

The County Championship match between Derbyshire and Warwickshire was unique in the annals of the competition as, at one stage in Warwickshire's first innings, father and son Walter and Bernard Quaife were batting together and facing the bowling of Billy Bestwick at one end and his son Robert at the other end. Walter Quaife scored 107 before Robert Bestwick bowled him, while Bernard scored 20. Warwickshire won by ten wickets.

THE FIRST

FAMILY WITH THREE GENERATIONS OF FIRST CLASS CRICKETERS

HONOURABLE AND REVEREND

E.V. BLIGH,

GENTLEMEN OF KENT V GENTLEMEN OF ENGLAND AT LORD'S CRICKET GROUND, ST JOHN'S WOOD ROAD, ST JOHN'S WOOD, MIDDLESEX, ENGLAND. MONDAY 3 JULY 1848;

L.E. BLIGH,

KENT V DERBYSHIRE AT MOTE PARK, WILLOW WAY, MAIDSTONE, KENT, ENGLAND. 22 JULY 1878;

A.S. BLIGH,

SOMERSET V DERBYSHIRE AT COUNTY GROUND, ST JAMES STREET, TAUNTON, SOMERSET, ENGLAND. WEDNESDAY 7 JUNE 1922.

The first family to supply three generations of First Class cricketers was the Blighs. Grandfather Edward Bligh made his debut in First Class cricket keeping wicket for the Gentlemen of Kent against the Gentlemen of England at Lord's. Batting at number ten, he scored 14 in the first innings and five in the second innings when he moved up to number seven. He took a catch in the first innings and made a stumping in the second, as Gentlemen of England won by five wickets. He played 40 First Class matches, the last in 1864. His Eton- and Cambridge-educated son Lodovick Bligh was the great-grandson of the 4th Earl of Darnley, who played for Kent in 1790. Lodovick was a fast bowler who made his first appearance for Kent away to Derbyshire, but he did not bowl and made nine and a duck with the ball. He appeared in ten First Class matches, the last in 1884. His top score was 20 and his best bowling was two for 36. Lodovick's son, Algernon, was, like his grandfather, an occasional wicketkeeper. In 1922, he opened the batting for Somerset and made six and five and Somerset won by 55 runs. Between 1922 and 1926 Algernon Bligh played 14 First Class matches for Somerset, with a highest score of 73 not out. He died at Minehead, Somerset on 27 December 1952.

THE ONLY
BOWLER TO HIT THE STUMPS FIVE TIMES WITH FIVE BALLS IN FIRST CLASS CRICKET

C.W.L. PARKER, GLOUCESTERSHIRE V YORKSHIRE AT FRY'S GROUND, NEVIL ROAD, BISHOPSTON, BRISTOL, GLOUCESTERSHIRE, ENGLAND. THURSDAY 10 AUGUST 1922.

The County Championship match between Gloucestershire and Yorkshire was designated as Charlie Parker's benefit match. In the White Rose County's first innings Parker took nine wickets for 36 as a Yorkshire side that included Percy Holmes, Herbert Sutcliffe and Wilfred Rhodes were dismissed for 66. Parker hit the stumps five times in consecutive balls but the umpire called his second delivery a no-ball and Parker had to be happy with a hat-trick. Yorkshire had their revenge by bowling out Gloucestershire for 58 and won the match by six wickets.

THE ONLY
BRITISH PRIME MINISTER TO PLAY FIRST CLASS CRICKET

LORD DUNGLASS, MIDDLESEX V OXFORD UNIVERSITY AT THE UNIVERSITY PARKS, PARKS ROAD, OXFORD, OXFORDSHIRE, ENGLAND. SATURDAY 3 MAY 1924.

Alexander Frederick Douglas-Home was born in London on 2 July 1903, the eldest son of Charles Cospatrick Archibald Douglas-Home, 13th Earl of Home. In 1918, on the death of his grandfather, he became Lord Dunglass, the courtesy title of the eldest son of the Earl of Home. He played cricket at Eton, taking four Harrow wickets for 37 at a rain-soaked Lord's in his last year before a crowd of about 20,000, when the fixture had social importance. He then went up to Christ Church, Oxford.

In the spring of 1924 Dunglass made his First Class debut for Middlesex against his university. He scored just one in the first innings and three in the second knock. He was the first change bowler for the county and took two for 23 and one for 28, as Middlesex won by 117 runs. Oddly, his second First Class match was for Oxford University. He toured South America with MCC. Lord Dunglass played ten First Class matches in total and made a highest score of 37 not out. With the ball, the best figures he returned were three for 43. He took 12 wickets.

In 1931 he was elected an MP and in February 1936 Dunglass was appointed parliamentary private secretary to Neville Chamberlain, then the Chancellor of the Exchequer. He stayed *in situ* when Chamberlain became premier. In July 1951 he became the 14th Earl of Home. On 27 July 1960 Harold Macmillan appointed Home Foreign Secretary. Three years later, he became Prime Minister, replacing Macmillan who was worn down by scandal. Sir Alec Douglas-Home, as he had become on renouncing his peerage, was only in Number 10 for a year before losing to Harold Wilson in 1964. When Ted Heath defeated Wilson in 1970, he reappointed Douglas-Home as Foreign Secretary, a job he held until 1974. The only Prime Minister to play First Class cricket, he died on 9 October 1995, aged 92.

━◆••◆━

THE ONLY
SOUTH AFRICAN TEST CRICKETER NEVER TO HAVE PLAYED FIRST CLASS CRICKET IN SOUTH AFRICA

G.M. Parker, South Africa v England at Edgbaston, Birmingham, Warwickshire, England. Saturday 14 June 1924.

George Parker appeared in two Tests for South Africa – the first two in the 1924 rubber in England. He is the only South African Test cricketer never to have played First Class cricket in South Africa. Born in Cape Town, he was playing in the Bradford League when a South African team short of bowlers called him into the Test side for the first Test and for what was only his second First Class match. In that game he took six for 152, including five wickets on the opening day, and was so exhausted that he had to leave the field. After the second Test, he never played First Class cricket again and eventually emigrated to Australia.

COMPLETED TEST INNINGS
IN WHICH NO PLAYER
REACHED DOUBLE FIGURES
SOUTH AFRICA v ENGLAND
AT EDGBASTON, BIRMINGHAM, WARWICKSHIRE, ENGLAND.
MONDAY 16 JUNE 1924.

There have been more than a dozen instances where a Test team has failed to make 50 but the only occasion on which none of the players reached double figures was on the second day of the first Test in 1924 when England, having made 438 all out (although, interestingly, no one made a century; Jack Hobb top scored with 76), bowled out South Africa for the pitifully low score of 30. Captain and opening batsman Herbie Taylor was the top scorer with seven. Arthur Gilligan took a Test career-best of six wickets for just seven runs, while his Sussex team-mate Maurice Tate took four for 12. They took just 75 balls and 48 minutes to bowl out the Springboks. South Africa made a fist of it in the second innings and scored 390 with Bob Catterall scoring 120, but it was not enough to prevent an England victory by an innings and 18 runs.

THE ONLY
TEST CRICKETER NEVER
TO BAT, BOWL OR TAKE A CATCH
J.C.W. MacBryan, England v South Africa at Old Trafford, Manchester, Lancashire, England. Saturday 26 July 1924.

Having already won the series against South Africa, England gathered at Old Trafford hoping to make it four victories in a row. The Springboks won the toss and elected to bat before 8,000 spectators. Torrential rain ended the day's play at 4 pm after 165 minutes, during which time South Africa made 116 for four. Rain prevented play on the rest of the scheduled days and opener Jack MacBryan's Test career began and ended. Slated to bat at number three, he is the only Test cricketer never to bat, bowl or take a catch.

THE FIRST
BATSMAN TO SCORE 4,000 TEST RUNS

J.B. HOBBS, ENGLAND V AUSTRALIA AT LORD'S CRICKET GROUND, ST JOHN'S WOOD ROAD, ST JOHN'S WOOD, MIDDLESEX, ENGLAND. MONDAY 28 JUNE 1926.

Jack Hobbs became the first batsman to score 4,000 runs in Test cricket. The momentous occasion happened during the second Test at Lord's when Hobbs had scored 83. He went on to score 119, as England made 475 for three declared in reply to Australia's 383 all out. Australia were on 194 for five when the match petered out into a draw. Fast bowler Harold Larwood marked his debut with three wickets (two in the first innings and one in the second).

THE FIRST
KNIGHTHOOD FOR SERVICES TO ANY SPORT

F.E. LACEY, 1926.

Sir Francis Lacey, the first man knighted for services to cricket, was born at Wareham, Dorset. He played football and cricket for Cambridge, obtaining a Blue for football in 1881 and one for cricket in 1882. A barrister by profession, he played for Hampshire. He scored 323 not out for Hampshire against Norfolk in 1887 in a non-First Class fixture, which remains the highest score ever made in a Minor Counties match. From 1898 to 1926 he was secretary of MCC. On his retirement, he became the first man knighted for services to any sport.

THE ONLY
PLAYER TO WIN
COUNTY CHAMPIONSHIP MEDALS,
TEST CAPS AND AN
FA CUP WINNER'S MEDAL
J.W.H. MAKEPEACE,

England v Scotland at Hampden Park, Mount Florida, Glasgow, Scotland.
Saturday 7 April 1906; Everton v Newcastle United at Crystal Palace, London,
England. Saturday 21 April 1906; England v Australia at Melbourne Cricket
Ground, Jolimont, Melbourne, Victoria, Australia. Friday 31 December 1920;
Lancashire, 1926, 1927, 1928, 1930.

Harry Makepeace was one of those rare people – a man who played
football and cricket for England. Born at Middlesbrough, Yorkshire on 22
August 1881, he played for Everton from 1906 until 1912. He made his
football debut for England on 7 April 1906 against Scotland in a match
that England lost 2-1. It was the first of four caps. A fortnight later, he
played for Everton in the FA Cup Final as they beat Newcastle United
1-0. On 26 July of the same year he made his First Class debut for
Lancashire against Essex at the County Ground, Leyton. A right-hand
batsman and leg-break bowler, he opened the batting and made 49 and five
and took one catch, as Lancashire won by 13 runs. It was the first of 499
First Class matches he played, the last beginning on 6 August 1930
against Middlesex.

On 20 April 1907 Makepeace returned to Crystal Palace and played
for Everton in the FA Cup Final against The Wednesday, but this time
ended up on the losing team as the Yorkshire side won 2-1. On
31 December 1920 he made his Test debut against Australia at Melbourne.
He scored four in both innings as Australia won by an innings and 91 runs.
His highest Test score was 117. He won the County Championship
with Lancashire on four occasions. He died at Bebington, Cheshire on
19 December 1952.

THE FIRST

BATSMAN TO SCORE 400 IN A FIRST CLASS INNINGS TWICE

W.H. PONSFORD, VICTORIA V QUEENSLAND AT MELBOURNE CRICKET GROUND, JOLIMONT, MELBOURNE, VICTORIA, AUSTRALIA. SATURDAY 17 DECEMBER 1927.

On 5 February 1923 Bill Ponsford became the first batsman to score 400 runs in a First Class match. The following day Victoria achieved the greatest winning margin in Australian cricket when they beat Tasmania by an innings and 666 runs at Melbourne Cricket Ground. Tasmania won the toss and decided to bat in the 'timeless' match and made 217 all out, Colin Newton, on an undefeated 49, the top scorer. Victoria then made 1,059 all out with captain Ponsford making 429. Tasmanian bowler Ashley Facy had his career figures wrecked by returning two for 228. A dispirited Tasmanian side was then all out for 176. Five players made their First Class debuts for Tasmania and seven for Victoria during the match. Nearly five years later, Ponsford bested his previous score to hit 437 against Queensland in the Sheffield Shield to become, not only the first batsman to score 400-plus twice, but also the only player to twice break the world record for the highest individual score in First Class cricket. Victoria won by an innings and 197 runs.

BILL PONSFORD WAS ALSO: The ONLY batsman to twice break the world record for the highest individual score in First Class cricket in 1932

THE FIRST

TEST MATCH FOR WEST INDIES

WEST INDIES V ENGLAND AT LORD'S CRICKET GROUND, ST JOHN'S WOOD ROAD, ST JOHN'S WOOD, MIDDLESEX, ENGLAND. SATURDAY 23 JUNE 1928.

West Indies played their first Test match at Lord's against England and the home side scored 382 runs on the first day, finally reaching 401. Ernest Tyldesley, in his first appearance in a Test at Lord's, scored 122 and

Learie Constantine took four for 82. The tourists made 177, with opening batsman Freddie Martin and wicketkeeper and captain Karl Nunes taking honours as top scorers, hitting 44 and 37 respectively. Vallance Jupp was England's bowling ace, taking four for 37. Fast bowler Harold Larwood missed the Windies second innings because of a strain, but even without him England wrapped up an innings victory before lunch on the final day, skittling out West Indies for 166.

THE ONLY
BOWLER TO TAKE
300 FIRST CLASS WICKETS
IN A SEASON
A.P. FREEMAN, ENGLAND. 1928.

One of the best leg-break bowlers the sport has ever seen, Freeman took 250 or more wickers in a season on six occasions – 1929 (267), 1930 (275), 1931 (276), 1932 (253) and 1933 (298) and 1928, when he took an incredible 304 wickets at a cost of 11,857 runs with an average of 18.05. He captured ten wickets in an innings on three occasions – 1929, 1930, and 1931. He took ten wickets in a match on 140 occasions. Born at Lewisham, south London on 17 May 1888, Alfred Percy 'Tich' was only 5 foot 2 inches (1.58 m) tall, hence his nickname. He was named *Wisden* Cricketer of the Year in 1923. Freeman died at Bearsted, Kent on 28 January 1965.

DUNBOWLIN'

When he retired 'Tich' Freeman opened a chain of sports goods shops with his former Kent team-mate Jack Hubble. Freeman called the house he lived in retirement Dunbowlin'.

THE FIRST

THE FIRST
BATSMAN UNDER 20
TO SCORE A TEST
HUNDRED

A. JACKSON, AUSTRALIA V ENGLAND AT ADELAIDE OVAL, WAR MEMORIAL DRIVE, NORTH ADELAIDE, SOUTH AUSTRALIA, AUSTRALIA. MONDAY 4 FEBRUARY 1929.

On his Test debut Archie Jackson opened the batting and scored 164 against England at the age of 19 years and 152 days, in the fourth, 'timeless' Test of the 1928–1929 rubber. Jackson played eight Tests and was regarded by many as someone who would have rivalled Don Bradman as Australia's greatest batsman. It was not to be. He contracted tuberculosis and died aged 23 on 16 February 1933, the day that England regained the Ashes in the Bodyline series.

THE FIRST
BATSMAN TO SCORE
5,000 TEST RUNS

J.B. HOBBS, ENGLAND V AUSTRALIA AT MELBOURNE CRICKET GROUND, JOLIMONT, MELBOURNE, VICTORIA, AUSTRALIA. THURSDAY 14 MARCH 1929.

Jack Hobbs became the first player to score 5,000 runs in Test cricket when he hit his 18th run in England's second innings against Australia. It was a day of records: at the age of 46 years and 82 days he became the oldest batsman to score a century in Test cricket. It was also the first Test to be played over eight days and the game in which Hobbs scored his 15th Test century. It was also his last Test Down Under.

THIS MATCH WAS ALSO: The FIRST Test to be played over eight days
• The LAST Test match Jack Hobbs played in Australia

THE LAST
PLAYER TO BOWL EIGHT BATSMEN
IN A FIRST CLASS INNINGS
G.O.B. ALLEN, MIDDLESEX V LANCASHIRE AT LORD'S CRICKET GROUND, ST JOHN'S WOOD ROAD, ST JOHN'S WOOD, MIDDLESEX, ENGLAND. SATURDAY 15 JUNE 1929.

Gubby Allen took all ten wickets for Middlesex against Lancashire for 40 runs and hit the stumps eight times. His other two victims were caught behind and stumped by wicketkeeper Fred Price. In the second innings, Allen took just one wicket for 65. The match ended in a draw.

THE FIRST
PLAYER TO TAKE A
HAT-TRICK
ON TEST DEBUT
M.J.C. ALLOM, ENGLAND V NEW ZEALAND AT LANCASTER PARK, CHRISTCHURCH, NEW ZEALAND. FRIDAY 10 JANUARY 1930.

Cambridge and Surrey amateur Maurice Allom played in just five Tests, four in New Zealand and one in South Africa, in 1930 and 1931 but was the first player to take a hat-trick on his debut and the first player to take four wickets in five balls. He made his Test debut in New Zealand's inaugural Test. In his eighth over Allom bowled Stewart Dempster with the second ball. His third delivery was missed by New Zealand captain Tom Lowry but Allom got him lbw with the fourth. The next victim was Ken James, caught behind by wicketkeeper Tich Cornford, and with the sixth ball Allom clean bowled Ted Badcock, giving him a hat-trick and four wickets in five balls. New Zealand collapsed to 21 for seven. They recovered to make 112 but still lost the match inside two days. Allom took five for 38 and three for 17. Six of England's players, including the captain Arthur Gilligan, were making their Test debuts in the match.

THIS MATCH WAS ALSO: The FIRST Test match for New Zealand
• The FIRST player to take four wickets in five balls

THE FIRST

TEST WIN FOR WEST INDIES

WEST INDIES V ENGLAND AT BOURDA, GEORGETOWN, BRITISH GUIANA. WEDNESDAY 26 FEBRUARY 1930.

West Indies won their first Test match when they beat England. The occasion was the third Test of the 1929–1930 series, held at Bourda, Georgetown, British Guiana. The Windies won the toss and elected to bat. They amassed 471 with a double century from Clifford Roach, who had scored a ton in the first match between the two countries before getting a pair in the second match. The West Indies then skittled England out for a meagre 145. A spirited fight back from England in their second innings was not enough to stop the home nation winning by 289 runs.

THE FIRST

PLAYER TO SCORE A TRIPLE TEST CENTURY

A. SANDHAM, ENGLAND V WEST INDIES AT SABINA PARK, KINGSTON, JAMAICA. SATURDAY 5 APRIL 1930.

England scored 849 in the fourth, 'timeless' Test against West Indies at Kingston, Jamaica – the highest innings total by any team in First Class cricket in the West Indies. Andy Sandham led the way with 325 – becoming the highest scorer in a Test innings – before being bowled by Herman Griffith, one of only two wickets he took in the innings. Les Ames hit a Test career-best 149 before he became Griffith's other victim. For West Indies Tommy Scott took a career-best five wickets for 266. The match finally ended with both teams agreeing to a draw after rain washed out the last two days' play. Sandham's record only lasted three months, until Don Bradman scored 334 against England at Headingley, Leeds in the third Test in July 1930. Bradman scored 309 of those runs on just one day – 11 July.

THE ONLY
BOWLER TO TAKE MORE THAN
4,000 FIRST CLASS WICKETS
W. RHODES, 1898–1930.

Wilfred Rhodes was born at Moor Top, Kirkheaton, Yorkshire on 29 October 1877 and, although he was a right-hand batsman, he bowled slow left arm. He made his First Class debut for Yorkshire in 1898 and the following year, on 1 June, appeared in the first of what would be 58 Test matches for England. In a career spanning 32 years Rhodes played 1,110 First Class matches and scored 39,969 runs (2,325 in Tests). He hit 58 centuries and 197 half-centuries. He took 4,204 runs (127 in Tests) at an average of 16.72. He took five wickets in an innings on 287 occasions and ten wickets in a match 68 times. On 16 occasions he took 100 wickets or more in a season. He also held 765 catches. He was the first England Test player to score 1,000 runs and take 100 wickets. At 52 years and 165 days, he was the oldest player to appear in a Test match. He went blind in 1952, after an unsuccessful operation for glaucoma, and died at Southmead, 159 York Road, Broadstone, Dorset on 8 July 1973 at the age of 95.

WILFRED RHODES WAS ALSO: The FIRST England Test player to score 1,000 runs and take 100 wickets in 1903

THE FIRST
TEST IN SOUTH AFRICA
PLAYED ON A GRASS WICKET
South Africa v England at Newlands, Cape Town, Western Cape, South Africa. Thursday 1 January 1931.

Having won the first Test of the 1930–1931 rubber, South Africa moved to Newlands where they played their first Test on a grass wicket. All the previous 40 Tests in South Africa had been played on matting wickets. The match ended in a draw, as did the rest of the Tests in the series.

PLAYER TO SCORE FOUR
TEST CENTURIES BEFORE HE TURNED 21

G.A. HEADLEY MBE, WEST INDIES. SATURDAY 17 JANUARY 1931.

George Alphonso Headley was born on 30 May 1909 at Colon, Panama where his father was helping to build the canal. He was taken to Jamaica when he was ten. He was planning to study dentistry in America but, while waiting for a passport, he played cricket against a touring English side, scoring 78 in the first match and 211 in the second. He made his Test debut for West Indies on 11 January 1930 and scored three centuries in that series. In 1931, on the second day of the third Test against Australia at the Exhibition Ground, Brisbane, Headley hit an unbeaten 102 to become the only player under 21 to score four Test centuries. (See 1948, page 129.)

BOWLER TO TAKE
ALL TEN WICKETS
IN FIRST CLASS CRICKET
ON THREE OCCASIONS

A.P. FREEMAN, KENT V LANCASHIRE AT MOTE PARK, WILLOW WAY, MAIDSTONE, KENT, ENGLAND. WEDNESDAY 24 JULY 1929; KENT V ESSEX AT SOUTHCHURCH PARK, NORTHUMBERLAND CRESCENT, SOUTHEND, ESSEX, ENGLAND. WEDNESDAY AUGUST 1930; KENT V LANCASHIRE AT OLD TRAFFORD CRICKET GROUND, STRETFORD, MANCHESTER, LANCASHIRE, ENGLAND. WEDNESDAY 27 MAY 1931.

'Tich' Freeman is the only bowler who has taken all ten wickets in an innings on three occasions, two of those occasions against Lancashire. In the first innings against Lancashire in 1929 his figures were 42-9-131-10. Yet Lancashire (347 and 305 for six declared) still beat Kent (235 and 228) by 189 runs. Freeman scored 28 and 11. The following season he bowled 30.4 overs against Essex which included eight maidens. He took all ten first innings wickets for 53 runs. Kent (122 and 422 for nine declared) beat

Essex (145 and 122) by 277 runs. In 1931 he again demolished Lancashire with figures of 36.1-9-79-10. The match ended in a draw. All of his ten-wicket hauls took place in the first innings.

—•◦•—

THE ONLY
FATHER AND SON TO SCORE CENTURIES IN THE SAME FIRST CLASS INNINGS

G. GUNN AND G.V. GUNN, NOTTINGHAMSHIRE V WARWICKSHIRE AT EDGBASTON, EDGBASTON ROAD, EDGBASTON, BIRMINGHAM, WARWICKSHIRE, ENGLAND. THURSDAY 23 JULY 1931.

For a son to follow in his father's footsteps is not unusual in any walk of life, and cricket is no exception. More than 200 sons have followed their fathers into First Class cricket, more than 20 into the Test arena, and there are at least eight English examples of families with three generations of First Class cricketers (see page 105). But what *is* unusual – in fact, unique – is for father and son both to score a century in the same innings.

When the Gunns did so in 1931, George Senior began his century innings at the age of 52 and ended it at the age of 53, causing discrepancies in a number of record books. *Wisden* described George Gunn as 'probably the greatest batsman who played for Nottinghamshire'. He was the most outstanding member of a cricketing family that included his brother John, son George Vernon and uncle William, all of whom played for the county.

George Senior was in the twilight of his illustrious career when he scored 77 not out on the second day of Nottinghamshire's 1931 match at Edgbaston. Play resumed on 24 July with Notts on 163 for one, chasing Warwickshire's 511 for three declared. Anyone who thought that the match was a lost cause hadn't counted on the Gunns. First, George celebrated his 53rd birthday by taking his score to 183, his penultimate century before retiring the following year with a record 583 appearances for Nottinghamshire. Then 26-year-old George Vernon took the crease and sealed a win for Notts by scoring the first of 11 First Class career centuries, ending the match on exactly 100 not out.

George Senior is also notable for being the player with the longest interval between Test match appearances for England, having waited 17 years and 316 days between playing for England against Australia in a match that ended on 1 March 1912 and being recalled on 11 January 1930, at the age of 51, to face West Indies.

Sadly George Vernon predeceased his father by eight months when he died on 15 October 1957 as a result of injuries that he sustained in a motorbike accident.

THE LAST
FIRST CLASS CENTURY BY JACK HOBBS

J.B. HOBBS, SURREY V LANCASHIRE AT OLD TRAFFORD, MANCHESTER, LANCASHIRE, ENGLAND. MONDAY 28 MAY 1934.

Jack Hobbs scored his 197th and last First Class century when he hit 116 while playing for Surrey against Lancashire at Old Trafford. At the time he was 51 years and 163 days old.

THE ONLY
ENGLAND TEST PLAYER JAILED FOR MANSLAUGHTER

V.W.C. JUPP, NORTHAMPTON ASSIZES, NORTHAMPTONSHIRE, ENGLAND. FRIDAY 25 JANUARY 1935.

In January 1935 England Test cricketer Vallance Jupp was convicted at Northampton Assizes of manslaughter and sentenced to nine months in jail. He had been driving his car on the wrong side of the road when he hit a motorcyclist, killing the pillion passenger. Jupp was released in early June 1935 after serving $4\frac{1}{2}$ months but did not resume his cricket career until 1936. He died in 1960.

THE FIRST
BOWLER TO TAKE
200 TEST WICKETS

C.V. Grimmett, Australia v South Africa at Old Wanderers, Johannesburg, Gauteng, South Africa. Monday 17 February 1936.

Born at Caversham, Dunedin, New Zealand on Christmas Day 1891, Clarrie Grimmett became the first player to take 200 wickets in Test cricket when he captured the wicket of Nipper Nicholson in Grimmett's 36th and penultimate Test. Grimmett was not happy to be discarded from the Test side, believing that he still had much to offer. No England bowler would take 200 wickets until 26 June 1953 ,when Alec Bedser achieved that feat. Grimmett died on 2 May 1980 at Adelaide, Australia.

THE FIRST
WICKETKEEPER TO MAKE
50 TEST STUMPINGS

W.A.S. OLDFIELD, AUSTRALIA V ENGLAND AT MELBOURNE CRICKET GROUND, JOLIMONT, MELBOURNE, VICTORIA, AUSTRALIA. TUESDAY 2 MARCH 1937.

Australian Bert Oldfield was the first wicketkeeper to stump 50 victims in Test cricket. He played 54 Tests and took 78 catches as well as the 52 stumpings. He made his Test debut on 17 December 1920 against England in the first Test match after the First World War. His first stumping victim was Johnny Douglas, the England captain. On 23 June 1934 he became the first wicketkeeper to claim 100 victims in Tests when he stumped Hedley Verity off the bowling of Clarrie Grimmett. His 50th stumping victim was Bill Voce in England's first innings for three off the bowling of Bill O'Reilly. Australia won the match by an innings and 200 runs and won the series 3-2 after having lost the first two matches. It was the first occasion a team had won a rubber after losing the first two games.

BERT OLDFIELD WAS ALSO: The FIRST wicketkeeper to claim 100 wickets in Tests

THE ONLY
PLAYER TO SCORE 3,000 RUNS
AND TAKE 100 WICKETS IN THE SAME SEASON
J.H. Parks, 1937.

In a feat that would be almost impossible to replicate today, James Horace Parks (1903–1980) scored 3,003 runs and took 101 wickets for Sussex in 35 matches in the 1937 season. He scored his 3,000th run on 4 September 1937 playing for the Over-30s against the Under 30s. Parks hit 61 to finish with an average 50.89. He hit 11 centuries and took 21 catches. Jim Parks came from a family of cricketers – his brother Harry played for Sussex, his son James Michael represented Sussex, Somerset and England and his grandson Bobby played for Hampshire (see 1980, page 179). In 1937 he made his only Test appearance, scoring 22 and seven and taking three wickets for 36 in the two innings at Lord's against New Zealand. Len Hutton made his debut in the same match. Hutton went on to appear in 78 more Tests and add another 6,970 runs to his career total. Another debutant in the match was Walter Hadlee, father of future Test cricketers Sir Richard and Dayle and One Day International player Barry Hadlee. Parks was a *Wisden* Cricketer of the Year in 1938. Parks's career ended with the Second World War.

—•••—

THE FIRST
TV BROADCAST OF A
CRICKET MATCH
England v Australia at Lord's Cricket Ground, St John's Wood Road, St John's Wood, Middlesex, England. Friday 24 June 1938.

The first televised cricket match was the second Test of the 1938 Ashes series. England captain Wally Hammond won the toss and elected to bat. England made 494, of which Hammond hit 240. Australia made 422 and opener Bill Brown carried his bat for 206. England declared their second innings at 242 for eight and when the match ended in a draw Australia were on 204 for six. The commentary on the BBC was by Captain Henry Blythe

Thornhill 'Teddy' Wakelam (1893–1963) who also commentated on the first football match broadcast on the wireless. He also commentated on rugby and boxing. John Arlott said of him, '[He was] a natural talker with a reasonable vocabulary... and a conscious determination to avoid journalese'.

THE ONLY
BATSMAN TO SCORE DOUBLE CENTURIES
IN BOTH INNINGS IN FIRST CLASS CRICKET
A.E. FAGG, KENT V ESSEX AT CASTLE PARK CRICKET GROUND, SPORTSWAY, CATCHPOLE ROAD, COLCHESTER, ESSEX, ENGLAND. WEDNESDAY 13 JULY 1938.

In the 1938 County Championship Arthur Fagg opened the innings for Kent and scored 244 in five hours in his first innings. In the second innings he was 202 not out, which took him two hours and 50 minutes. His second innings opening partnership with Peter Sunnucks reached 283.

THE FIRST
BATSMAN TO SCORE
350 IN A TEST
L. HUTTON, ENGLAND V AUSTRALIA AT THE OVAL, KENNINGTON, SURREY, ENGLAND. TUESDAY 23 AUGUST 1938.

In the match that saw England achieve their biggest ever Test victory over Australia – an innings and 579 runs. England won the toss and elected to bat, with Len Hutton and Bill Edrich opening for the home side. Hutton stayed at the crease for 13 hours and 17 minutes to make 364 – then the highest innings in a Test match – before being out. Maurice Leyland, in his last Test, hit 187, completing a partnership of 382 with Hutton. Joe Hardstaff was 169 not out when captain Wally Hammond declared at 903 for seven. For Australia captain Don Bradman and batsman Jack Fingleton were missing, both injured, as the tourists tumbled to 201 all out before Hammond enforced the follow-on. They fared even less well in the second innings when they were dismissed for 123 (only one extra – a bye – added to their total).

THE FIRST
BATSMAN TO SCORE
6,000 TEST RUNS

W.R. Hammond, England v South Africa at Old Wanderers, Johannesburg, Gauteng, South Africa. Saturday 24 December 1938.

On the first day of the first Test of the 1938–1939 rubber between South Africa and England Wally Hammond, the England captain, became the first player to score 6,000 runs in Test cricket. He made just 24 but it was enough to send him past the milestone as England reached 422 all out. The Springboks replied with 390 before England declared on 291 for four. When play finished on 28 December the match was drawn. On 19 August 1946 at The Oval, playing against India, Hammond achieved another milestone and became the first player to score 7,000 Test runs. (See 1939, page 124.)

WALLY HAMMOND WAS ALSO: The FIRST player to score 7,000 Test runs

THE ONLY
FIELDER TO TAKE
MORE THAN 1,000 CATCHES
IN A CAREER

F.E. Woolley, 1906–1938.

Frank Edward Woolley was born at Tonbridge, Kent on 27 May 1887 and made his debut for his county in 1906 becoming one of the finest all-rounders off all time. Woolley is the only non-wicketkeeper to have held more than 1,000 catches, finishing with 1,018. He scored 58,969 First Class runs – second only to Jack Hobbs. Woolley shares with W.G. Grace the record of having made 1,000 runs in a season 28 times. Woolley also took 2,068 wickets and played 64 Test matches between 1909 and 1934. His first and last Tests were against Australia at The Oval. He died on 18 October 1978 at Chester, Nova Scotia, Canada. Woolley Road in Maidstone, Kent is named for him.

THE ONLY

TEN-DAY
FIRST CLASS MATCH

SOUTH AFRICA V ENGLAND AT KINGSMEAD, DURBAN, KWAZULU-NATAL, SOUTH AFRICA. FRIDAY 3 MARCH 1939.

The 'timeless' Test between South Africa and England finally came to an end after ten days, 43 hours and 16 minutes, the longest First Class match ever played. It only ended because the English tourists had to leave to catch the boat home. South Africa won the toss and batted first. They made 530 all out with two centenarians – Pieter van der Bijl (125 – his highest Test score) and Dudley Nourse (103) – and three other players hitting half-centuries. Reg Perks took five Springbok wickets for 100 – his best Test figures. England were then dismissed for 316, with wicketkeeper Les Ames top scoring on 84.

The Springboks made 481 in their second innings with captain Alan Melville hitting 103 after openers van der Bijl (97) and Bruce Mitchell put on 191 for the opening wicket. England were set a target of 696 to win and were just 42 short of victory when rain forced the match to be abandoned. There was also no play owing to rain on 11 March. Paul Gibb made 120 – his best Test score – and captain Wally Hammond 140 but there was only one double centenarian (Bill Edrich who hit 219 in England's second innings). The match saw 1,981 runs scored for the loss of 35 wickets – an average of just under 57 runs per wicket.

—◆•◆—

THE FIRST
FIELDER (EXCLUDING WICKETKEEPER)
TO TAKE 100 TEST CATCHES

W.R. Hammond, England v West Indies at Old Trafford, Manchester, Lancashire, England. Tuesday 25 July 1939.

Wally Hammond made his debut on Christmas Eve 1927 against South Africa at Old Wanderers, Johannesburg. He became the first fielder to hold 100 catches in Test cricket when he caught George Headley at slip in the second Test against West Indies at Manchester. His ton came up in 76 Tests. In all, Hammond played 85 Tests, his last in 1947, and scored 7,249 runs at an average of 58.45. He also took 83 wickets, averaging 37.40 and finished with 110 catches. (See 1938, page 123.)

THE ONLY
SEASON WHEN EIGHT-BALL OVERS
WERE USED IN ENGLAND
1939.

Since 1902 six-ball overs have been the norm in England, except for one season – 1939 – when an experiment was conducted using eights balls per over. The idea was to have a two-year experiment with the new number of deliveries but the Second World War intervened and when hostilities ceased English cricket returned to six-ball overs.

THE ONLY
AUSTRALIAN TO SCORE A CENTURY
IN EACH INNINGS OF HIS
DEBUT FIRST CLASS MATCH

A.R. MORRIS, NEW SOUTH WALES V QUEENSLAND AT SYDNEY CRICKET GROUND, MOORE PARK, MOORE PARK ROAD, SYDNEY, NEW SOUTH WALES, AUSTRALIA. SATURDAY 28 DECEMBER 1940.

Arthur Morris, a month away from his 19th birthday, became the only Australian to score a century in each innings of his debut First Class match when he hit a nelson (111) against Queensland at Sydney Cricket Ground. A left-hander, he had scored 148 in the first innings and his runs helped New South Wales to win by 404 runs. He went on to play 46 Test matches for Australia with a highest score of 206.

AN UNFORTUNATE PASSER-BY

There have been a number of spectators who have died during the course of a match. However, in 1731 a Mr Legat was walking by the Artillery Ground in London when he was hit on the nose by a cricket ball. 'When the bleeding stopt outwardly he bled inwardly and when stopt inwardly, he bled outwardly' – the unfortunate passer-by died on 6 July 1731 from loss of blood.

THE ONLY
PLAYER TO HAVE DIED DURING A MATCH AT LORD'S

A. DUCAT, LORD'S CRICKET GROUND, ST JOHN'S WOOD ROAD, ST JOHN'S WOOD, MIDDLESEX, ENGLAND. THURSDAY 23 JULY 1942.

Surrey Test batsman Andrew Ducat died of a heart attack while batting for Surrey Home Guard against Sussex Home Guard at Lord's. A former Arsenal midfielder, he was one of the few people to have represented England at international level at both football and cricket. He was 56.

THE LAST
SURVIVOR OF THE FIRST TEST MATCH
T.W. GARRETT, FRIDAY 6 AUGUST 1943.

Tom Garrett died at Warrawee, Sydney, Australia, aged 85 years 11 days. He was the last surviving player from the first Test match in March 1877. An all-rounder, he played 19 Tests, scoring 339 runs with a top score of 51 not out. He took 36 wickets with an innings best of six for 78 and a match best of nine for 163. In the first Test he scored 18 not out and nought. He was one of Australia's opening bowlers in the match and he took two for 22 and nought for nine.

POST-SECOND WORLD WAR TEST

NEW ZEALAND V AUSTRALIA AT BASIN RESERVE, WELLINGTON, NEW ZEALAND. FRIDAY 29 MARCH 1946.

The first Test match after the Second World War was played between New Zealand and Australia over two days at Wellington. Australia fielded seven debutants while the Kiwis had six new players. New Zealand, captained by Walter Hadlee, won the toss and elected to bat. They were no match for the Australians and were bowled out for just 42. Only two of the Kiwis made a double-figure score. Tiger O'Reilly took five for 14 and Ernie Toshack four for 12 while Ray Lindwall took the remaining Kiwi wickets. When they batted Australia made just 199, with captain Bill Brown top scoring with 67 and Sid Barnes making 54. The most successful Kiwi bowler was Jack Cowie who took six for 40. When they resumed on day two the match was over by 3.35 pm when New Zealand were all out for 54. Again, just two players scored double figures – this time five Australian bowlers shared the spoils as the Aussies won by an innings and 103 runs.

MAN TO PLAY TEST CRICKET FOR
ENGLAND
AND INDIA

NAWAB OF PATAUDI SENIOR, ENGLAND V AUSTRALIA AT SYDNEY CRICKET GROUND, MOORE PARK, MOORE PARK ROAD, SYDNEY, NEW SOUTH WALES, AUSTRALIA. FRIDAY 2 DECEMBER 1932; INDIA V ENGLAND AT LORD'S CRICKET GROUND, ST JOHN'S WOOD ROAD, ST JOHN'S WOOD, MIDDLESEX, ENGLAND. SATURDAY 22 JUNE 1946.

The only man to play Test cricket for England and India, the senior Nawab of Pataudi, Iftikhar Ali Khan, was born at Pataudi, Punjab on 16 March 1910. Having won a Blue at Oxford, he was selected for the England squad for the 1932–1933 Bodyline series. He scored a century (102) on his Test debut but was dropped after the second Test after he criticized captain

Douglas Jardine's tactics and returned to England before his team-mates. He was a *Wisden* Cricketer of the Year in 1932. He played once more for England, also against Australia, in 1934 but then did not play Test cricket again until 1946 when he was captain of India for three matches against England. Apart from his first innings, he never managed to recapture his First Class form on the Test arena and averaged only 19.90. His First Class average was 48.61. He retired for reasons of ill health and was only 41 when he died on 5 January 1952 of a heart attack while playing polo.

THE FIRST
OFFICIAL DEFINITION
OF FIRST CLASS CRICKET
Thursday 19 May 1947.

In 1947 The Imperial Cricket Conference defined the term 'First Class' and declared that 'a match of three or more days' duration between two sides of 11 players officially adjudged First Class, shall be regarded as a First Class fixture. Matches in which either team has more than 11 players or which are scheduled for less than three days shall not be regarded as First Class. The governing body in each country shall decide the status of the teams.'

THE ONLY
BOWLER TO DISMISS
DON BRADMAN HIT WICKET
L. AMARNATH, INDIA V AUSTRALIA AT BRISBANE CRICKET GROUND, VULTURE STREET, WOOLLOONGABBA, BRISBANE, QUEENSLAND, AUSTRALIA. MONDAY 1 DECEMBER 1947.

In the first Test of the 1947–1948 rubber Australia won the toss and elected to bat in their first-ever Test match against India. Australian captain Don Bradman batted for all of the first day but only an hour's play was possible on the second. On the third day he was out on 185 hit wicket, bowled by India captain Lala Amarnath, the only instance of Bradman being out in that fashion. It didn't help much – Australia made 382 for eight declared and then bowled out India for 58 and 98 to win by an innings and 226 runs. Amarnath top scored with 22 in India's first innings – 37.93 per cent of his country's total.

THE FIRST

BLACK MAN TO CAPTAIN

A WEST INDIES TEST TEAM

G.A. Headley, West Indies v England, at Kensington Oval, Bridgetown, Barbados. Wednesday 21 January 1948.

George Headley became the first black man to captain West Indies, when he led the side against England in the first Test of the 1947–1948 rubber at Kensington Oval, Bridgetown, Barbados. (See 1931, page 117.)

THE ONLY

FIRST CLASS PLAYER WITH

MORE THAN 50 LETTERS

IN HIS NAME

ILIKENA LASARUSA TALEBULAMAINAVALENIVEIVAKABULAIMAINAKULALAKEBALAU, FIJI V AUCKLAND AT EDEN PARK, AUCKLAND, NEW ZEALAND. FRIDAY 13 FEBRUARY 1948.

Ilikena Talebulamainavaleniveivakabulaimainakulalakebalau played in nine First Class matches for Fiji, beginning in 1948 and ending in 1954. He was born on 15 November 1921 at Tobou, Fiji and his name means 'returned alive from Nankula hospital at Lakemba island in the Lau group'. Luckily for scorers, he was happy for his name to be abbreviated to I.L. Bula.

THE LAST

TEST APPEARANCE BY DON BRADMAN

**Australia v England at The Oval, Kennington, Surrey, England.
Saturday 14 August 1948.**

Don Bradman played his last innings for Australia, against England at The Oval and received a standing ovation from the crowd and players as he made his way to the middle. He needed just four runs to retire with a Test batting average of 100. However, Eric Hollies had other ideas and bowled Bradman second ball for a duck. Bradman finished on an average of 99.94. Bradman claimed that he could not see properly because he had tears in his eyes, although England wicketkeeper Godfrey Evans disputed that. And Hollies was most upset: 'My best ball of the bloody season and they're clapping him!'

THE ONLY

TEST MATCH DECIDED ON THE LAST DELIVERY

**SOUTH AFRICA V ENGLAND AT KINGSMEAD, DURBAN, KWAZULU-NATAL, SOUTH AFRICA, MONDAY
20 DECEMBER 1948.**

England beat South Africa in the first Test of the 1948–1949 rubber – the only time a Test has been decided on the last ball. South Africa won the toss and decided to bat. They made 161 with Alec Bedser taking four for 39. England replied with 253 all out, with Len Hutton top scorer on 83. Top wicket-taker was Tufty Mann (who would die of cancer just four years later at the tragically young age of 31) with six for 59. In their second innings the Springboks made 219. England progressed steadily but needed eight runs from the last eight-ball over for victory. At the crease were Alec Bedser and Cliff Gladwin and bowling for the Springboks was Lindsay Tuckett. Bedser levelled the scores off the sixth ball but then Gladwin missed the seventh delivery. It was down to the last ball. Gladwin missed again but the ball hit his thigh and he and Bedser rushed a leg bye to ensure victory for England.

THE ONLY

AUSTRALIAN CRICKETER
TO BE KNIGHTED

SIR DONALD BRADMAN, SATURDAY 1 JANUARY 1949.

Australia's legendary batsman Don Bradman is the only Australian cricketer to be knighted. A year after his gong, Bradman published his autobiography, *Farewell to Cricket*. After his cricket career ended, Bradman became a stockbroker but retired in June 1954 and concentrated on earning money as a director of various companies. He also became a cricket consultant and Test selector. On 16 June 1979 the Australian government awarded Bradman the Companion of the Order of Australia 'in recognition of service to the sport of cricket and cricket administration'.

THE ONLY

TEST CRICKETER
TO WIN AN FA CUP WINNER'S MEDAL

D.C.S. COMPTON, ARSENAL V LIVERPOOL AT WEMBLEY STADIUM, MIDDLESEX, ENGLAND. SATURDAY 29 APRIL 1950.

Denis Compton, the first sportsman to advertise Brylcreem, spent the whole of his cricket career with Middlesex and the whole of his football career at Arsenal. He joined the MCC ground staff at Lord's in 1934. Four years later, he scored his first Test century against Don Bradman's touring Australia. He played 78 Tests, scoring 5,807 runs with an average of 50.06 and hit 17 centuries with a highest score of 278. A winger, he made his debut for the Gunners in 1936 and won the League in 1948 and FA Cup in 1950. By the 1950 Final, when he appeared against Liverpool, he was already into his 30s, inclined to run out of puff and troubled by a notorious knee injury. In the first half, in his own words, he 'played a stinker'; in the second, fuelled by a mammoth slug of whisky administered by Alex James, he put in a dazzling performance. With brother Leslie, the Comptons are the only brothers to play in the same

County Championship and Football League Championship winning sides. They played for Middlesex in 1947 and Arsenal in 1947–1948.

DENIS AND LESLIE COMPTON WERE: The ONLY brothers to play in the same County Championship and Football League Championship winning sides

THE ONLY
SEPTUAGENARIAN
FIRST CLASS CRICKETER
R.M. SINGH, BOMBAY GOVERNOR'S XI V COMMONWEALTH XI AT BRABOURNE STADIUM, BOMBAY, INDIA. SATURDAY 25 NOVEMBER 1950.

Raja Maharaj Singh was the captain of the Bombay Governor's XI in their match against the touring Commonwealth XI. The Commonwealth included Les Ames, Sonny Ramadhin, Jim Laker, Eddie Paynter and Derek Shackleton. Playing in his only First Class match was Raja Maharaj Singh who was an incredible 72 years old at the time. Bombay Governor's XI won the toss and decided to bat. They were dismissed for 202 with their skipper contributing four. Commonwealth XI declared at 483 for five. The excitement and his age proved too much for Singh, who was absent for the Bombay Governor's XI's second innings. Without him, they were bowled out for 108 and Commonwealth XI won by an innings and 173 runs.

THE ONLY
MAN TO PLAY WORLD CUP FOOTBALL
AND TEST CRICKET FOR ENGLAND
W. Watson, England v Ireland at Maine Road, Moss Side, Manchester, Lancashire, England. Wednesday 16 November 1949; England v South Africa at Trent Bridge, Nottingham, Nottinghamshire, England. Thursday 7 June 1951.

Born on 7 March 1920 at Bolton on Dearne, Yorkshire, Willie Watson is the only man to have played in a World Cup match for England and also Test cricket for England. A left-handed batsman, he made his debut for

Yorkshire on 22 July 1939 against Nottinghamshire at Bramall Lane, Sheffield, only to have his career interrupted by the Second World War. He resumed his career when peace was proclaimed.

He made 223 League appearances for Sunderland in seven seasons at Roker Park. He made his international football debut (one of four appearances for his country) in the first World Cup qualifying home match played by England, a 9-2 victory over Ireland at Maine Road. However, he did not appear in any matches played during the final stages of the World Cup in Brazil in 1950. The following year he made his Test debut against South Africa, the first of 23 appearances. He scored 109 over almost six hours in the second Test in 1953 at Lord's against the Australians when the match appeared all but lost. He was not picked for The Oval Test when the Ashes were regained after 19 years. In 1954 he was named as one of *Wisden*'s five Cricketers of the Year.

That year he became manager of Halifax Town, a position he held until 1956. In 1958 he left his native county and joined Leicestershire CCC as assistant secretary and captain. He retired in 1962, though he made nine appearances in 1963 and 1964. That was the year he undertook a second spell as manager at Shay Ground which lasted two years. From 1966 until 1968 he was manager of Bradford City. He died on 23 April 2004.

THE FIRST
TEST BATSMAN DISMISSED
FOR OBSTRUCTING THE FIELD
L. HUTTON, ENGLAND V SOUTH AFRICA AT THE OVAL, KENNINGTON, SURREY, ENGLAND. SATURDAY 18 AUGUST 1951.

Len Hutton became the first batsman dismissed for obstructing the field in a Test match. England were chasing a target of 163 to beat South Africa in the fifth Test and Hutton had scored 27 when he top-edged a ball from off-spinner Athol Rowan and, to stop it from hitting the stumps, he played at it a second time but in doing so he stopped debutant wicketkeeper Russell Endean from taking a catch. It didn't matter too much in the end – England won by four wickets. (See 1957, page 141.)

THE FIRST
TEST WIN BY
INDIA

India v England at M.A. Chidambaram Stadium, Chepauk, Madras, India. Sunday 10 February 1952.

India won their first Test match when they beat England by an innings and eight runs at M.A. Chidambaram Stadium, Chepauk, Madras. It was their 25th attempt at winning a Test. The arrangements for the match were changed when King George VI died on the first day and the rest day was moved to the second day. The hero of the match for India was Vinoo Mankad, who took eight for 55 in England's first innings, scored 22, and took four for 53 in the second innings as India won the match within four days.

THE ONLY
WISDEN CRICKETER OF THE YEAR
NOT TO RECEIVE AN OBITUARY
IN THE ALMANACK

J.T. NEWSTEAD, BLACKBURN, LANCASHIRE. TUESDAY 25 MARCH 1952.

The only *Wisden* Cricketer of the Year who did not receive an obituary in the almanack was John Thomas 'Jack' Newstead who died at Blackburn, Lancashire, aged 74. Newstead was selected for the honour in 1909 after a spectacular season for Yorkshire the year before, when he took 140 wickets, at 16.50 each, and scored 927 runs. His form declined in 1910 and he was dropped from the Yorkshire side but, had there been a Test series in 1908, it is likely that he would have made at least one international appearance. *Wisden* rectified their earlier omission 42 years later when Newstead appeared as a supplementary obituary in the 1994 almanack.

THE FIRST

PROFESSIONAL
ENGLAND
TEST CAPTAIN
L. HUTTON, ENGLAND V INDIA

AT HEADINGLEY, ST MICHAEL'S LANE, LEEDS, YORKSHIRE, ENGLAND. THURSDAY 5 JUNE 1952.

Len Hutton became the first professional England Test captain when he led the team out against India in the first Test at Headingley. India won the toss and elected to bat and made 293 all out with Jim Laker taking four for 39. England made 334 with Tom Graveney the top scorer on 71. India then made Test history by losing their first four wickets in the first 14 deliveries without scoring.

THE ONLY

TEST SIDE DISMISSED
TWICE IN
THE SAME DAY

INDIA V ENGLAND AT OLD TRAFFORD, MANCHESTER, LANCASHIRE, ENGLAND. SATURDAY 19 JULY 1952.

In 1952 India became the only Test side dismissed twice in the same day. In the third Test against England, the home team declared at 347 for nine with captain Len Hutton scoring 104. England's Freddie Trueman then bowled out India for 58 with only two players making double figures. Trueman's figures were eight for 31. India went into bat again and this time made 82 with Alec Bedser and Tony Lock taking nine wickets between them and Trueman only taking one, thus failing to get ten wickets in a match. England won the match by an innings and 207 runs.

THE FIRST

TEST WIN BY
PAKISTAN

PAKISTAN V INDIA AT UNIVERSITY GROUND, LUCKNOW, INDIA. SUNDAY 26 OCTOBER 1952.

Pakistan won a Test match for the first time when they beat India at University Ground, Lucknow in the second game of the 1952–1953 rubber. Of the five matches, India won two and two were drawn. For this milestone Test India won the toss, decided to bat and were dismissed for 106. Fazal Mahmood took five for 52. Pakistan made 331 and Nazar Mohammad carried his bat for 124 in an innings that lasted eight hours and 35 minutes. India were all out for 182 in their second innings and Fazal Mahmood took seven for 42, to give him a match analysis of 12 for 94.

THE FIRST

PROFESSIONAL ENGLISH CRICKETER
TO BE KNIGHTED

SIR JOHN BERRY HOBBS, 1953.

Jack Hobbs made his First Class debut for Surrey at The Oval against the Gentlemen of England, captained by W.G. Grace, on 24 April 1905. Hobbs scored the highest individual score in both innings 18 and 88. They were the first of 61,237 First Class runs, which included 199 centuries, scored by The Master. In 1921 he was taken ill during the Headingley Test match and his life was saved by an emergency operation for an ulcerated appendix. In 1923 he became only the third player to make a century of centuries. England regained the Ashes after 14 years at The Oval in 1926, with Hobbs making exactly 100. That year he became the first professional to be a Test selector. He played 61 Tests, hitting 15 centuries and scoring 5,410 runs (average 56.94). He retired with 197 centuries under his belt, although some insisted on including tons he had scored on a private tour of India – Hobbs refused to countenance this. The statisticians credited him with 244 centuries at all levels. In 1949, he was made a life member of MCC and in 1953 he became the first professional English cricketer to be knighted. Jack Hobbs died at his home in his sleep on 21 December 1963.

JACK HOBBS WAS ALSO: The FIRST professional cricketer to be a Test selector

THE FIRST
FIVE-TEST SERIES TO FINISH WITH FIVE DRAWS
PAKISTAN V INDIA AT PAKISTAN. TUESDAY 1 MARCH 1955.

On 1 March 1955 the fifth Test ended between Pakistan and India in a draw, as indeed had the previous four in the rubber – the first time all five Tests in a series had been drawn.

THE ONLY
TEST CRICKETER TO BE EXECUTED
L.G. Hylton, St Catherine's Prison, St Catherine, Jamaica, West Indies. Tuesday 17 May 1955.

Wisden's obituary of West Indies fast bowler Leslie Hylton makes no mention of the nature of his demise, stating merely that he 'died in Jamaica on May 17, 1955, aged 50'. But Hylton did not simply die; he was hanged for the murder of his wife, Lurlene. Leslie George Hylton is the only Test cricketer to have been hanged for murder.

A fast bowler, he was born on 29 March 1905 . His debut Test match was against England in Barbados when he took three wickets for eight runs in the first innings. He made six appearances for West Indies between 1935 and 1939 and helped to win the rubber against R.E.S. Wyatt's touring side in 1934–1935, taking 13 wickets in four Tests at an average of 19.30. In 1939 he was not included in the side to visit England under R.S. Grant and a public appeal raised £400 to pay for his fare. It turned out to be a waste of money. Hylton took just three wickets in two Tests. His top Test score was 19. He also played 40 First Class matches for his native Jamaica, top scoring with 80 and taking 120 wickets.

In 1954 Hylton's wife Lurlene confessed to adultery with a notorious womanizer called Roy Francis. She said to her cuckolded husband one night, 'I'm in love with Roy. My body belongs to him.' Hylton shot her seven times, then telephoned the police. At his trial his counsel, his Jamaican cricket captain Noel 'Crab' Nethersole, produced a letter Lurlene had written to Roy Francis. 'My beloved,' it said, 'I'm realizing even more than I did before how much I love you. I am going to force my man's hand as soon as I can.' Nethersole further claimed that Hylton was attempting to shoot himself but missed. Lack of accuracy was perhaps not the most credible defence for a former Test bowler with an average of 26.6, particularly given that he would have had to stop to reload his revolver, but it still took the all-male jury fully an hour and a half to convict. While in the death cell Hylton was received into the Roman Catholic Church.

THE FIRST
NON-MUSLIM TO PLAY
TEST CRICKET FOR PAKISTAN
W. MATHIAS, PAKISTAN V NEW ZEALAND AT DACCA STADIUM, EAST PAKISTAN. MONDAY 7 NOVEMBER 1955.

The Roman Catholic Wallis Mathias became the first non-Muslim to represent Pakistan at Test level when he made his debut against New Zealand. The match was something of a washout with no play on three of the five days. The Kiwis were bowled out for just 70 in their first innings while Pakistan made 195 for six declared, with Mathias scoring an unbeaten 41. New Zealand were on 69 for six when the match was abandoned as a draw. Mathias played in 21 Tests over the next seven years and excelled in the slips, taking 22 catches, although his batting figures in Tests did not do justice to his talent. He scored 783 runs at an average of 23.72, whereas his First Class average was 44.49 from 146 matches and 7,520 runs. In 1963 he injured his finger in the nets, which left him with a deformed hand, making it difficult for him to catch the ball. He retired during the 1975–1976 season.

THE ONLY
TEST MATCH IN WHICH BATSMEN AVERAGED OVER 100 RUNS PER WICKET LOST

NEW ZEALAND V INDIA AT FEROZ SHAH KOTLA, DELHI, INDIA. FRIDAY 16 DECEMBER 1955.

The third Test in the 1955–1956 rubber saw New Zealand bat first after winning the toss. They made 450 for two declared (Bert Sutcliffe 230 not out, John Reid 119 not out). India replied with 531 for seven declared (Vijay Manjrekar 177) and New Zealand were on 112 for the loss of one wicket when the match ended in a draw.

THE FIRST
TEST WIN BY NEW ZEALAND

NEW ZEALAND V WEST INDIES AT EDEN PARK, AUCKLAND, NEW ZEALAND.
TUESDAY 13 MARCH 1956.

New Zealand won a Test match for the first time when they beat West Indies in the fourth Test at Eden Park, Auckland, by 190 runs. It was the first victory in 26 years and 45 matches and followed three successive defeats in the rubber. The Kiwis, captained by John Reid, won the toss and chose to bat, making 255, with Reid leading the way with 84. Tom Dewdney took five for 21. In their first innings the West Indians made 145 (Hammond Furlonge 64, Tony MacGibbon four for 44, Harry Cave four for 22). New Zealand declared at 157 for nine (captain Denis Atkinson seven for 53) and then demolished the tourists, skittling them out for 77 (Cave four for 21) not long after tea on the fourth day. Locally, offices closed early and excited workers rushed to the ground to see Harry Cave and Don Beard bowl the Kiwis to their first victory.

THE ONLY
SIDE TO WIN A FIRST CLASS MATCH
IN ENGLAND
WITHOUT LOSING A WICKET

Lancashire v Leicestershire at Old Trafford, Manchester, Lancashire, England. Saturday 14 July 1956.

Lancashire beat Leicestershire in the County Championship at Old Trafford without losing a wicket. Leicestershire won the toss and decided to bat. They were all out for 108 with Brian Statham taking four for 32. In reply Lancashire made 166 for nought declared, the runs coming from Alan Wharton (87) and Jack Dyson (75). Leicestershire made 122 in their second innings with Malcolm Hilton taking five for 23. Lancashire then made 66 for nought to win the match by ten wickets.

THE ONLY
PLAYER TO TAKE
ALL TEN WICKETS IN A TEST INNINGS

J.C. LAKER, ENGLAND V AUSTRALIA AT OLD TRAFFORD, MANCHESTER, LANCASHIRE, ENGLAND. TUESDAY 31 JULY 1956.

By the end of 1956 the Australians must have dreaded the sight of Jim Laker. In May, playing for Surrey against the tourists, Laker took all ten wickets for just 88 runs, making Surrey the first county for 44 years to beat the Australians and Laker the first bowler for 78 years to take ten Australian wickets in an innings. Two months later he did it again, achieving two cricketing firsts by becoming the first player to take all ten wickets in a First Class innings twice in the same season, and the first player to take all ten wickets in a Test match. More than 50 years later he remains the only player to have achieved either. During the 1956 Test series as a whole Laker took 46 wickets for an average of just 9.6 runs but, compared with his performance in the fourth Test, even this remarkable series record pales into insignificance.

Victory in the fourth Test at Old Trafford would secure the series for England, who scored 459 in the first innings. Australia then made 48 before Laker took the first two wickets. Tony Lock took the third and Laker the remaining seven in 22 balls for just eight runs – the Australians had gone from 48 for nought to 84 all out, and Laker's figures were nine for 37 in just eight overs. Lock's wicket had prevented Laker from achieving the magic ten in an innings, but not for long. Australia followed on, hoping to save the match and the series. Laker took his first wicket on day two and his second on day three, despite only 45 minutes' cricket being played that day due to bad weather. Continuing bad weather gave the Aussies a chance to hold out for a draw, and they began the final day with eight wickets intact. At lunch Australia still had eight wickets. By tea Laker had taken four of them. After tea Laker took four more, the last of them at 5.27 pm with just 33 minutes of play remaining.

Thus Jim Laker became the first player to take all ten wickets in a Test innings, and for just 53 runs. His overall match figures were an amazing 19 for 90, and the next day's headlines were no exaggeration: 'Laker defeats Australia by an innings and 170 runs'. But the story would not be complete without Laker's own recollection of his drive home from Old Trafford. In his memoirs, *Over to Me*, he describes stopping for a beer and a cheese sandwich at a pub in Lichfield, Staffordshire. There he listened to the regulars marvelling at his 19 wickets, none of them realizing that he was sitting among them.

—◆—◆—

THE FIRST
TEST BATSMAN GIVEN OUT
HANDLED THE BALL

W.R. ENDEAN, SOUTH AFRICA V ENGLAND AT NEWLANDS, CAPE TOWN, WESTERN CAPE, SOUTH AFRICA. SATURDAY 5 JANUARY 1957.

South Africa's Russell Endean became the first batsman in Test cricket given out handled the ball. The incident occurred on the morning of the final day of the second Test. South Africa had begun the day on 41 for two

---

MOHINDER AMARNATH

On 9 February 1986 Mohinder Amarnath of India became the first batsman to be dismissed for handling the ball in One Day Internationals. He was on 15 at Melbourne Cricket Ground in the second match between Australia and India. Australia won by seven wickets with 16 balls remaining.

---

with Endean not out on three. He was unable to add to his overnight tally when he was out in the most unusual fashion trying to fend off a delivery from Jim Laker. (See 1951, page 133.)

THE FIRST
EDITION OF TEST MATCH SPECIAL

BBC THIRD PROGRAMME AT EDGBASTON, EDGBASTON ROAD, EDGBASTON, BIRMINGHAM, WARWICKSHIRE, ENGLAND. THURSDAY 30 MAY 1957.

The first edition of *Test Match Special* began with the England v West Indies Test match at Edgbaston, Birmingham. The BBC advertised the new programme with the slogan, 'Don't miss a ball. We broadcast them all.' *TMS* began on the Third Programme before switching to the Light Programme at 5.15 pm. As for the Test, it ended as a draw with the most memorable event being a 411-run partnership between captain Peter May (285) and Colin Cowdrey (154) for the fourth wicket. *TMS* was broadcast for 30 years on Radio 3 before moving to Radio 4 in 1994. Brian Johnston joined the team from television in 1970 and was known as much for his giggling and bestowing of nicknames to his colleagues as for his commentaries.

THE FIRST
WICKETKEEPER TO TAKE 200 TEST DISMISSALS

T.G. Evans, England v West Indies at Headingley, St Michael's Lane, Leeds, Yorkshire, England. Saturday 27 July 1957.

England's Godfrey Evans became the first wicketkeeper to make 200 dismissals in Test cricket when he caught Collie Smith off the bowling of Don Smith in West Indies' second innings of the fourth Test at Headingley, Leeds. It was Evans's 80th Test.

THE LAST
MAN TO PLAY CRICKET & FOOTBALL FOR ENGLAND

C.A. MILTON, ENGLAND V AUSTRIA AT WEMBLEY STADIUM, MIDDLESEX, ENGLAND. WEDNESDAY 28 NOVEMBER 1951; ENGLAND V NEW ZEALAND AT HEADINGLEY, ST MICHAEL'S LANE, LEEDS, YORKSHIRE, ENGLAND. SATURDAY 5 JULY 1958.

Arthur Milton was born at Bedminster, Somerset on 10 March 1928 and made his debut for Gloucestershire against Northamptonshire on 2 June 1948 at County Ground, Northampton. He was eight not out in his one innings as the match ended in a draw. In 1950 he joined Arsenal and played 75 League matches for the Gunners scoring 18 goals. He made just one appearance for England in a 2-2 draw against Austria in the 1951–1952 season.

In the summer of 1958 he made his first Test appearance at Headingley in the third Test against New Zealand. He carried his bat for 104 and took two catches as England won by an innings and 71 runs. Milton became the first Gloucestershire player since W.G. Grace to score a century on his Test debut. He was also the first England player to be on the pitch for the whole of a Test match, a record he retained until 1986–1987. He did not play in the fourth Test but returned in the fifth and scored 36. It was enough to get him on the Ashes tour of 1958–1959 but he struggled against the

Aussies. He played in six Tests: two each against New Zealand, Australia and India. He retired in 1974, having scored 32,150 runs (and 56 hundreds). In retirement he became a postman in the Cotswolds, maintaining his fitness by jumping on and off his bicycle during his rounds.

ARTHUR MILTON WAS ALSO: The FIRST England player to be on the pitch for the whole of a Test match

THE FIRST
TELEVISED TEST MATCH
IN AUSTRALIA

AUSTRALIA V ENGLAND AT BRISBANE CRICKET GROUND, VULTURE STREET, WOOLLOONGABBA, BRISBANE, QUEENSLAND, AUSTRALIA. FRIDAY 5 DECEMBER 1958.

The first televised Test match in Australia was the contest between the old enemies. Australia (186 and 147 for two) beat England (134 and 198) by eight wickets at the Gabba. The Test was also notable for England's Trevor Bailey taking seven hours and 38 minutes to score 68 in the second innings. The knock included just four fours. Peter May set a Test record by captaining England for the 26th time.

THE LAST
WHITE MAN TO CAPTAIN THE
WEST INDIES TEST TEAM

F.C.M. ALEXANDER, WEST INDIES V PAKISTAN AT NATIONAL STADIUM, KARACHI, PAKISTAN. FRIDAY 20 FEBRUARY 1959.

Wicketkeeper Franz Copeland Murray 'Gerry' Alexander became the last white man to date to captain the West Indies Test team when he led them in the first Test against Pakistan at the National Stadium, Karachi. Alexander had made his Test debut under John Goddard at Headingley, Leeds in 1957 and played just two Tests before being given the captaincy. West Indies won seven, lost four and drew seven of his 18 Tests in charge.

THE FIRST

PLAYER TO BAT ON ALL FIVE DAYS OF A TEST MATCH

M.L. JAISIMHA, INDIA V AUSTRALIA AT EDEN GARDENS, CALCUTTA, INDIA. THURSDAY 28 JANUARY 1960.

Motganhalli Jaisimha made 39 Test appearances for India and scored more than 2,000 runs. Subsequently there have been four other players who have also batted on every day: Geoff Boycott, Kim Hughes, Allan Lamb and Ravi Shastri.

THE LAST

FIRST CLASS MATCH TO
FINISH ON THE FIRST DAY

KENT V WORCESTERSHIRE AT NEVILL GROUND, TUNBRIDGE WELLS, KENT, ENGLAND. WEDNESDAY 15 JUNE 1960.

Colin Cowdrey called the pitch at the Nevill Ground, Tunbridge Wells 'disgraceful' as the County Championship match between Kent and Worcestershire was wrapped up inside a day. Kent batted first and made 187 all out, with Peter Jones the top scorer with 73. Worcestershire then made 25 in 17.1 overs with no player getting out of single figures and six of them recording a duck. Alan Brown took six for 12. In their second knock Worcestershire more than doubled their score, hitting 61 and David Halfyard taking five for 20 as Kent won by an innings and 101 runs.

THE FIRST

TIED TEST MATCH

AUSTRALIA V WEST INDIES AT BRISBANE CRICKET GROUND, VULTURE STREET, WOOLLOONGABBA, BRISBANE, QUEENSLAND, AUSTRALIA. WEDNESDAY 14 DECEMBER 1960.

The first tied game in Test cricket occurred between Australia, led by Richie Benaud, and West Indies, under the captaincy of Frank Worrell, at the Brisbane Cricket Ground. West Indies won the toss and elected to

TIED AGAIN

A Test was tied for only the second time in 1,052 matches, on 22 September 1986 when India played Australia at M.A. Chidambaram Stadium, Chepauk, Madras. Australia won the toss and decided to bat. Australia made 574 for seven when captain Allan Border declared. Dean Jones had scored 210, David Boon 122 and Border himself 106. India were bowled out for 397 with captain Kapil Dev scoring 119. Greg Matthews took five for 103. Border declared the second Australian knock on 170 for five, leaving India the target of 348 to win in 87 overs. The Indians set about their task with skill and pace – but at 5.18 pm, with one run needed for victory in the fifth ball of Greg Matthews's 40th over, he trapped the Indian number 11 Maninder Singh lbw leaving the scores tied, both teams having scored 744 runs.

bat making 453 with Gary Sobers hitting 132. Australia made 505 with Norm O'Neill hitting a Test best of 181 and Wes Hall taking four for 140. In their second innings the Windies hit 284, leaving Australia 233 to win in 310 minutes. They were 232 for eight before wicketkeeper Wally Grout was run out on two. Last man Lindsay Kline came in with just one run needed but, as he and Ian Meckiff went for it, Meckiff, too, was run out on two, leaving the scores tied.

THE ONLY
PLAYER TO TAKE A WICKET WITH
HIS FIRST BALL IN BOTH INNINGS
OF FIRST CLASS DEBUT
R.V. WEBSTER, SCOTLAND V MCC AT GLENPARK, BRISBANE STREET, GREENOCK, RENFREWSHIRE, SCOTLAND. WEDNESDAY 14 JUNE 1961.

Rudi Webster was a fast bowler who was born at Marchfield, St Philip, Barbados on 10 June 1939. He made his First Class debut for Scotland against MCC and with his first ball took the wicket (bowled) of Dickie Dodds of Essex for nine, finishing with figures of seven for 56. In the second innings he captured the wicket (also bowled) of Arthur Phebey for a duck. He finished with 11 for 100 as Scotland won by 194 runs.

THE LAST

NORTH v SOUTH MATCH

North v South at Stanley Park, Blackpool, Lancashire, England. Friday 8 September 1961.

The last full-scale North v South match took place in 1961, the popularity of the competition waning as the public preferred Test matches. North won the last toss and decided to bat, making 216 all out. Top scorer was Lancashire's Brian Booth with 62 while Middlesex captain and leg-break bowler Ian Bedford took five wickets for 88 (just five years before his untimely death from a heart attack at the age of 36). South made 261 for eight declared, helped by 118 from Roger Prideaux. The North scored 324 all out in their second innings although no player scored a century. Glamorgan's Peter Walker took five for 102 which included his 100th wicket in First Class cricket. South reached their target hitting 283 for eight to win the match by two wickets. Wicketkeeper Godfrey Evans was unbeaten on 98. A 50-over North v South match was held in 1971 at Nottingham and was won by nine runs by South. It was far from being North v South in reality, as most of the North players actually played for counties in the Midlands.

THE FIRST

LIMITED OVERS COMPETITION IN ENGLISH CRICKET

MIDLANDS KNOCK-OUT COMPETITION. MAY 1962.

The Midlands Knock-Out Competition was the first limited overs competition in English cricket, although only Derbyshire, Leicestershire, Northamptonshire and Nottinghamshire took part. Each side was allocated 65 overs. The first ball in limited overs cricket in England was bowled at Trent Bridge at 11 am on 2 May 1962 by John Cotton of Nottinghamshire to Mick Norman of Northamptonshire, who became the first victim and the first duck. At the same time, across the Midlands, Les Jackson of Derbyshire bowled to Maurice Hallam of Leicestershire who scored 88, the highest score until the first century was scored in the Gillette Cup the following year. Northamptonshire became the first (and only) winners of the Midlands Knock-Out Competition when they beat Leicestershire at Grace Road, Leicester by five wickets on 9 May 1962.

THIS MATCH ALSO INCLUDED: The FIRST duck in limited overs cricket in England

THE LAST

CENTURY IN GENTLEMEN v PLAYERS

K.F. BARRINGTON, PLAYERS V GENTLEMEN AT NORTH MARINE ROAD GROUND, SCARBOROUGH, YORKSHIRE, ENGLAND. SATURDAY 8 SEPTEMBER 1962.

The Gentlemen v Players – amateurs and professionals – began in 1806 (the Gentlemen won) and the last match was played in September 1962 after which the amateur status was abolished. Six players, including Bill Edrich and Wally Hammond, played for both sides. Hammond was the only man to captain both sides to victory at Lord's – in 1937 for the Players and in 1938 for the Gentlemen. The penultimate game was played at Lord's and ended in a draw.

The Gentlemen batted first in the last game and made 328. Tony Lock took four for 68. The Players were all out for 377 with Ken Barrington scoring exactly 100. In their second innings the Gentlemen scored 217 with Freddie Trueman taking four for 11. South African Ray White was the top scorer with 95. The Players made 212 for three to win the last match by seven wickets. In total there were 137 Gentlemen v Players matches. The Players won 68, the Gentlemen 41 and 28 ended in a draw. On three occasions W.G. Grace scored a century and took ten wickets for the Gentlemen. He played in 85 of the matches and his nearest rival was Jack Hobbs, who appeared in 49. (See 1806, page 38.)

THE FIRST
ORDAINED MINISTER
TO PLAY TEST CRICKET
THE REVEREND D.S. SHEPPARD, ENGLAND V AUSTRALIA AT BRISBANE CRICKET GROUND, VULTURE STREET, WOOLLOONGABBA, BRISBANE, QUEENSLAND, AUSTRALIA. FRIDAY 30 NOVEMBER 1962.

The Reverend David Sheppard was the first ordained minister to play Test cricket. He had made his debut in 1950, five years before he was ordained into the Anglican Church. In 1954 he was captain for two Tests against Pakistan, but his clerical duties took up much of his time and he disappeared from the Test scene. He was recalled in 1962 against Pakistan and did well enough to be included on the Ashes winter tour. Opening the batting for England, Sheppard scored 31 and 53. His Test career ended in 1963 and he went on to become Bishop of Woolwich and Bishop of Liverpool before his death from bowel cancer on 5 March 2005.

THE LAST
TEST WICKET WITH
THE LAST TEST BALL
A.K. DAVIDSON, AUSTRALIA V ENGLAND AT SYDNEY CRICKET GROUND, MOORE PARK, MOORE PARK ROAD, SYDNEY, NEW SOUTH WALES, AUSTRALIA. 20 FEBRUARY 1963.

In the fifth Test of the 1962–1963 rubber between Australia and England at Sydney, two Australian stalwarts ended their careers.

Left-handed all-rounder Alan Davidson played 44 Tests, beginning in June 1953 against England. He was often stricken with injuries and in the fourth Test of his final series he tore his hamstring muscle after bowling only 3.4 overs and conceding 30 runs. The fifth Test was on his home ground at Sydney and the series was tied at one victory each. His final knock with the bat saw him score 15 before he was caught off the bowling of England captain Ted Dexter. In the first innings he took three for 43. In England's second knock he took three for 80 and with his final ball in Test cricket he captured the wicket of Alan Smith, caught at slip by Bob

Simpson. Australia were set a target of 241 in 60 overs but when the match ended in a draw they were on 152 for four. Davidson was a selector for the Australian team from 1979 to 1984.

The other player to retire from international cricket the same day was Neil Harvey, who appeared in 79 Tests and top scored with 205 from a total of 6,149 runs. He took three wickets with a best of one for eight. He was vice-captain from 1957 until his retirement. Harvey was named as one of *Wisden*'s Cricketers of the Year in 1954 and in 2009 was one of the 55 inaugural inductees into the ICC Cricket Hall of Fame.

THE FIRST

PLAYER TO SCORE
2,000 RUNS AND TAKE 200 WICKETS
IN TEST MATCHES

R. BENAUD, AUSTRALIA V SOUTH AFRICA AT BRISBANE CRICKET GROUND, VULTURE STREET, WOOLLOONGABBA, BRISBANE, QUEENSLAND, AUSTRALIA. FRIDAY 6 DECEMBER 1963.

Richie Benaud, doyen of Australian television commentators, was the first player to achieve the double double of 2,000 runs and 200 wickets in Test matches. It was in his 32nd Test (against South Africa at St George's Park, Port Elizabeth) that he achieved his first double. He was named as one of *Wisden*'s Cricketers of the Year in 1962. Benaud had made his Test debut ten years earlier, on 25 January 1952, against West Indies, and appeared in 63 Tests, scoring 2,201 runs with a top score of 122. He took 248 wickets with his best figures being seven for 72.

Benaud's double double occurred in the first Test of the 1963–1964 rubber against the Springboks. It was also Benaud's last Test match as

---

NO-BALLED

In the match which ended in a draw Australian left arm fast bowler Ian Meckiff announced his retirement from all cricket after he was no-balled four times for throwing in his only over of the Test, in which he conceded eight runs. He played 18 Tests for his country.

Australia's captain before he relinquished the skipper's job to Bob Simpson. The second man to achieve the double double was West Indian Sir Gary Sobers and the third England's Sir Ian Botham (in his 42nd Test).

THIS MATCH WAS ALSO: The LAST Test match in which Richie Benaud captained Australia

THE LAST

BOWLER TO TAKE TEN WICKETS
IN A FIRST CLASS INNINGS IN ENGLAND

N.I. THOMSON, SUSSEX V WARWICKSHIRE AT MANOR SPORTS GROUND, BROADWATER ROAD, WORTHING, WEST SUSSEX, ENGLAND. SATURDAY 6 JUNE 1964.

Medium fast bowler Ian Thomson took all Warwickshire's wickets in a County Championship match for 49 runs. He took five for 26 in the second innings but could not stop Warwickshire winning by 182 runs.

THE FIRST

BOWLER TO TAKE 300 TEST WICKETS

F.S. Trueman, England v Australia at The Oval, Kennington, Surrey, England. Saturday 15 August 1964.

Frederick Sewards Trueman began his Test career against India in 1952 and, because there was much less cricket played then, it took him 12 years to take his 300th wicket. The wicket was that of Neil Hawke for 14, caught by Colin Cowdrey. By the time 'Fiery Fred' retired he had taken 307 wickets at an average of 21.57. His record stood until 31 January 1976 when West Indian Lance Gibbs broke it at the Melbourne Cricket Ground. On 27 December 1981 Australia's Dennis Lillee had Larry Gomes caught at slip by Greg Chappell to overhaul Gibbs's record. Coincidentally, Lillee broke the record also at the Melbourne Cricket Ground.

THE ONLY
FIRST CLASS MATCH
IN WHICH ALL 22 PLAYERS BOWLED

A.E.R. Gilligan's XI v Australians at Central Recreation Ground, Hastings, Sussex, England. Wednesday 2 September 1964.

The Australian tourists began a three-day match against A.E.R. Gilligan's XI at the Central Recreation Ground, Hastings. A.E.R. Gilligan's XI batted first and made 372, including 119 from Basil D'Oliveira. The Australians were all out for 281 with Jim Pressdee taking five for 83. A.E.R. Gilligan's XI declared their second innings on 251 for nine, Michael Norman top scoring on 81. Thanks to a century from Bill Lawry, Australia made 346 for eight to win the match by two wickets. It was the only First Class game in which all 22 players took a turn at bowling.

THE ONLY
ANIMAL LISTED IN
WISDEN'S BIRTHS AND DEATHS
PETER THE LORD'S CAT, APRIL 1965.

Peter the Lord's cat died aged 14 on Thursday 5 November 1964. He lived for 12 years at the home of cricket and could often be seen prowling the outfield, especially during big matches. The secretary of the MCC said, 'He was a cat of great character and loved publicity.'

THE LAST
TEST APPEARANCE BY FRED TRUEMAN
ENGLAND V NEW ZEALAND AT LORD'S CRICKET GROUND, ST JOHN'S WOOD ROAD, ST JOHN'S WOOD, MIDDLESEX, ENGLAND. TUESDAY 22 JUNE 1965.

Yorkshire and England fast bowler 'Fiery Fred' Trueman finished his international career when he played his 67th and last Test for England. In 127 innings Trueman delivered 15,178 balls and took 307 wickets at a cost of 6,625 runs, with an average of 21.57. His innings best was eight for 31, while his match best was 12 for 119. In his final Test appearance, the second of three matches against New Zealand, he took two for 40 and nought for 69 and scored three runs as England beat the Kiwis by seven wickets. Trueman's last Test victim was Richard Collinge, bowled for seven. Trueman's last match also marked the Test debut of fast bowler John Snow.

THE ONLY
TEST BATSMAN TO HIT 50 BOUNDARIES IN AN INNINGS

J.H. EDRICH, ENGLAND V NEW ZEALAND AT HEADINGLEY, ST MICHAEL'S LANE, LEEDS, YORKSHIRE, ENGLAND. THURSDAY 8 JULY 1965.

Batting at Headingley, John Edrich hit an unbeaten 310 for England against New Zealand in an innings that lasted 532 minutes. Edrich hit five sixes and 52 fours as England declared on 546 for four. They then bowled out New Zealand for 193 and 166, having enforced the follow-on. England won by an innings and 187 runs.

THE LAST
ENGLAND-SOUTH AFRICA TEST BEFORE THE BAN

ENGLAND V SOUTH AFRICA AT THE OVAL, KENNINGTON, SURREY, ENGLAND. THURSDAY 26 AUGUST 1965.

In 1965 England played their last Test match against South Africa for 28 years, ten months and 21 days. The game at The Oval was the third and final in a three-match rubber (New Zealand had also toured earlier in the summer). The Springboks won the series 1-0, thanks to a 94-run victory in the second Test at Trent Bridge earlier in the month. England captain Mike Smith won the toss and invited the South Africans to bat first. The

Springboks made 208 (Tiger Lance 69, Brian Statham five for 40, debutant Ken Higgs four for 47) and 392 (Colin Bland 127, Higgs four for 96) while England replied with 202 (Colin Cowdrey 58, Peter Pollock five for 43) and 308 for four (Cowdrey 78 not out, Ken Barrington 73, Eric Russell 70).

Tours for 1968–1969 and 1970 were abandoned because of political pressure and in 1970 England played the Rest of the World in an unofficial series that was quickly put together. At the time players were awarded Test caps but the ICC later stripped the series of its Test status.

THE ONLY
PLAYER TO SCORE 2,000 FIRST CLASS RUNS IN THE SAME SEASON WITHOUT HITTING A CENTURY
D.M. GREEN, LANCASHIRE, ENGLAND. 1965.

David Green scored 2,037 runs for his county in the 1965 season at an average of 32.85 but, remarkably, did not achieve a three-figure innings total. He hit 40 or more on 20 occasions but could not get past 85. In 1968 he again scored more than 2,000 runs in a season, totalling 2,137, and his top score was 233. He was a *Wisden* Cricketer of the Year in 1969. He also played rugby union for Sale. On his retirement he became a cricket and rugby correspondent for *The Daily Telegraph*.

THE FIRST
COUNTY CHAMPIONSHIP MATCH PLAYED ON THE SABBATH
ESSEX V AUSTRALIA AT VALENTINE'S PARK, 27–37 PERTH ROAD, ILFORD, ESSEX, ENGLAND. SUNDAY 15 MAY 1966.

Essex played Somerset in the County Championship at Ilford, the first time that a match in the tournament had taken place on the Sabbath. The law prevented Essex from charging for admission but the 6,000 spectators contributed £500 in collections and by buying scorecards.

THE ONLY
FIRST CLASS CRICKETER
TO HAVE WON A FOOTBALL
WORLD CUP WINNER'S MEDAL

G.C. Hurst, England v West Germany at Wembley Stadium, Middlesex, England. Saturday 30 July 1966.

Sir Geoff Hurst excelled at both cricket and football. He signed for Essex and played only one First Class match for the county before deciding that football was his natural métier. His one appearance came at Aigburth, Liverpool on 30 May 1962 against Lancashire. It wasn't exactly a terrific performance by Hurst. Batting at number ten in the first innings and at number eight in the second, he was nought not out in the first innings and bowled for a duck in the second innings. He didn't bowl but he did take a catch to dismiss Tommy Greenough off the bowling of Jim Laker for five. Essex won by 28 runs but never picked Hurst again.

THE FIRST
WICKETKEEPER TO SCORE A CENTURY
AND MAKE FIVE DISMISSALS
IN A TEST INNINGS

D.T. LINDSAY, SOUTH AFRICA V AUSTRALIA AT NEW WANDERERS STADIUM, JOHANNESBURG, GAUTENG, SOUTH AFRICA. FRIDAY 23 DECEMBER 1966.

During the first Test of the 1966–1967 rubber between South Africa and Australia at New Wanderers Stadium, Johannesburg, Springbok wicketkeeper Denis Lindsay became the first man to score a century and make five dismissals in a Test innings. He held six catches in the first innings (eight catches in the match) and scored 182 in the second innings to add to the 69 he had scored in the first. To add to his triumph, South Africa won by 233 runs. The feat of two fifties and seven or more catches would not be repeated until April 2009, by Mahendra Dhoni for India against New Zealand.

THE LAST

BOWLERS TO BOWL UNCHANGED

IN BOTH COMPLETE

FIRST CLASS INNINGS

B.S. CRUMP AND R.R. BAILEY, NORTHAMPTONSHIRE V GLAMORGAN AT SOPHIA GARDENS, CARDIFF, GLAMORGAN, WALES. WEDNESDAY 7 JUNE 1967.

The last time two bowlers bowled unchanged in both innings of a First Class match was at Sophia Gardens, Cardiff between Northamptonshire and Glamorgan, when Brian Crump (five for 45 and seven for 29) and Ray Bailey (five for 64 and three for 31) helped Northants to a win by 132 runs.

THE ONLY

TIME TEN CATCHES

WERE TAKEN BY

TEN DIFFERENT

FIELDERS

LEICESTERSHIRE V NORTHAMPTONSHIRE AT GRACE ROAD, LEICESTER, LEICESTERSHIRE, ENGLAND. THURSDAY 31 AUGUST 1967.

The only instance of ten different fielders taking a catch in a First Class match occurred on the second day of the County Championship game between Leicestershire and Northampton. The only Leicestershire player not to take a catch was Jack Birkenshaw. He did take three wickets for 60, but was outclassed by his captain Tony Lock who took seven for 75. Disappointingly, in their second innings only four players were needed to dismiss Northamptonshire as Leicestershire won by 163 runs.

THE LAST

PLAYER TO DO THE DOUBLE – 1,000 RUNS AND 100 WICKETS IN THE SAME SEASON

F.J. TITMUS, 1967.

Middlesex's Fred Titmus was the last player to score 1,000 runs and 100 wickets in the same season. In 1967 he scored 1,093 runs at an average of 36.43 and took 196 wickets, averaging 20.35 runs. In 1969 the County Championship programme was reduced by four matches per county, making it almost impossible that anyone will achieve this feat again.

THE FIRST

PLAYER TO SCORE SIX SIXES IN A FIRST CLASS OVER

G.S. SOBERS, NOTTINGHAMSHIRE V GLAMORGAN AT ST HELEN'S, SWANSEA, WALES. SATURDAY 31 AUGUST 1968.

Gary Sobers is bemused by the excitement surrounding his legendary six sixes. 'Nobody talks about anything else,' he said 30 years later. 'At times I have to say, "You know, it seems as though the only thing I have ever done in cricket is hit six sixes."' But there's little wonder people remember it. It's the Everest of batting, cricket's four-minute mile. It is the perfect score – a first that cannot be bettered, and a feat that has only been matched once in more than 40 years since. The second and last player to date to score six sixes in a First Class over was Ravi Shastri, in 1985.

Sobers was captaining Nottinghamshire against Glamorgan and was about to declare, telling his batting partner John Parkin, 'I think we'll have another ten minutes.' Then Malcolm Nash bowled the first ball of what was to become the most famous over in cricket. Sobers walloped it out of the ground. The second ball went the way of the first, hitting the upper storey of a house in Gorse Lane, alongside the ground. BBC Wales commentator Wilf Wooller said drily: 'Glamorgan could do with a few

FIVE SIXES

In 1977 Malcolm Nash, fed up with being reminded of his humiliation at the bat of Sobers, boldly declared that it could never be done again. Shortly afterwards, Frank Hayes of Lancashire hit him for five sixes in the same over – 6, 4, 6, 6, 6, 6.

fielders stuck on top of that wall over there.' When the third ball went into the member's enclosure, Glamorgan captain Tony Lewis warned Nash to play it safe. But Nash dropped the next ball short and Sobers hooked it into the crowd behind him.

One of the Glamorgan slips told Sobers, 'I bet you can't hit the next one for six.' Sobers replied, 'Ah, that's a challenge,' and duly hit the ball long and high. Roger Davis caught it but fell backwards over the boundary. The previous season Sobers would have been out, but a new rule, introduced earlier in 1968, meant that it was yet another six. Almost as soon as the bat connected with the sixth ball, Wilf Wooller knew that history had been made – 'And he's done it! He's done it!' he cried. 'And my goodness, it's gone all the way down to Swansea.' In fact the ball landed, appropriately enough, in the garden of The Cricketers pub, where it was found the following day by a schoolboy and later presented to Sobers.

RAVI SHASTRI WAS: The LAST player to score six sixes in a First Class over

THE LAST
TEAM TO WIN THE COUNTY CHAMPIONSHIP
THREE TIMES IN A ROW
YORKSHIRE. 1966–1968.

Since there are only 18 First Class counties, one would imagine that winning the County Championship three times consecutively would be a regular occurrence. In fact, it has not happened for more than 40 years. Brian

Close led the White Rose County to the title in 1963 and again from 1966 to 1968. In November 1970 Close was sacked after a disagreement with the Yorkshire committee. Since 2000 the County Championship has been divided into two divisions. Sussex and Durham have both won the First Division twice but no side has yet won it three times in a row.

THE FIRST
TEST MATCH ABANDONED
DUE TO RIOTING
PAKISTAN V ENGLAND AT NATIONAL STADIUM, KARACHI, PAKISTAN. SATURDAY 8 MARCH 1969.

The third Test between Pakistan and England was abandoned when the crowd rioted shortly before lunch on the third day. England won the toss, decided to bat and were 502 for seven, with wicketkeeper Alan Knott needing only four for a maiden Test century, when the game ended in a draw.

THE LAST
APARTHEID-SOUTH AFRICA
TEST MATCH
SOUTH AFRICA V AUSTRALIA AT CRUSADERS GROUND, ST GEORGE'S PARK, PORT ELIZABETH, EASTERN CAPE, SOUTH AFRICA. TUESDAY 10 MARCH 1970.

South Africa beat Australia for the fourth time in the four-Test series that was to be their last international outing for 22 years, as they became the outcasts of international sport. The Springboks won by 323 runs at Crusaders Ground, Port Elizabeth, to go with their previous victories of winning by 170 runs, by an innings and by 129 runs and 307 runs. How good this team was and what they could have achieved will, sadly, never be known. Up until their exclusion, South Africa had played 172 Tests and played their last on the same ground that they had played their first, almost exactly 81 years earlier. (See 1889, page 72.)

THE FIRST
LIMITED OVERS INTERNATIONAL
MATCH

AUSTRALIA V ENGLAND AT MELBOURNE CRICKET GROUND, JOLIMONT, MELBOURNE, VICTORIA, AUSTRALIA. THURSDAY 5 JANUARY 1971.

Australia and England contested the first limited overs international match when the old enemies met at Melbourne Cricket Ground. The game was an impromptu one, played on what should have been the last day of the third Test (abandoned due to rain), and was billed as Australians v MCC. Each side was allowed to bowl 40 eight-ball overs but, in the end, neither side needed their full allocation. England scored 190 all out off 39.4 overs, while the Australians scored 191 for five off 34.6 overs. John Edrich, who opened the batting for England and scored 82, was the first Man of the Match.

THE ONLY
TEST CRICKETER RUN OUT IN THREE
CONSECUTIVE INNINGS

J.A. Jameson, England v India at Old Trafford, Manchester, Lancashire, England. Monday 9 August 1971; England v India at The Oval, Kennington, Surrey, England. Thursday 19 August 1971, Monday 23 August 1971.

John Jameson made his debut for England in the second Test of the 1971 rubber against India and in his first innings scored 15, opening the batting with Brian Luckhurst. In the second innings Jameson was run out for 28. His run of bad luck continued in the third and final Test of the series. He was on 82 and looking good for his maiden Test century when he was run out. His hat-trick of run-outs came in the second innings, when he was on 16. He did not play for England again until the 1973–1974 tour of the West Indies when he dropped down the order to number three and, although he was never run out again, he never got that elusive century.

THE ONLY

PLAYER TO SCORE A CENTURY IN BOTH INNINGS ON TEST DEBUT

L.G. ROWE, WEST INDIES V NEW ZEALAND AT SABINA PARK, KINGSTON, JAMAICA, MONDAY 21 FEBRUARY 1972.

Laurence Rowe became the first and, to date, only player to score a century in both innings of his Test debut. Batting at number three, he made 214 in the first innings, out of a West Indies total of 508 for four declared. In the second innings he made 100 without defeat. The match ended in a draw. Rowe was one of only two West Indies players who did not bowl in the match, the other being wicketkeeper Mike Findlay.

THE FIRST

BENSON & HEDGES CUP FINAL

Leicestershire v Yorkshire at Lord's Cricket Ground, St John's Wood Road, St John's Wood, Middlesex, England. Saturday 22 July 1972.

Running from 1972 until 2002, the Benson & Hedges Cup was the longest-running sponsored event in English First Class cricket. It was a limited overs (55, later reduced to 50) league competition followed by a knockout stage. The inaugural year featured all 17 First Class counties, plus Minor Counties South, Minor Counties North and Cambridge University. Oxford University participated in the second year and from 1976 both universities, together with other universities, contributed players to supply a Combined Universities team. In 1980 Scotland began playing and the Minor Counties were reduced to one team.

The first matches were played on 29 April 1972. However, because of bad weather, none was completed that day. In fact, it took three days to complete the one-day matches. On 13 May 1972 Leicestershire became the first team to score 300 in a Benson & Hedges Cup innings when they hit 327 for four against Warwickshire at Coventry. Michael Norman and

Brian Davison of Leicestershire became the first batsmen to share a 200 partnership – 227 for the third wicket. The first Final was held at Lord's between Yorkshire and Leicestershire, who won the toss and decided to field. After their allotted overs, Yorkshire had made 136 for nine with their top score coming from Barrie Leadbeater. Leicestershire needed only 46.5 of their overs to score 140 for five and win by five wickets.

On 30 April 1977 Yorkshire's Geoff Boycott became the first batsman to score 1,000 runs in Benson & Hedges Cup ties. The feat came in his 24th match, which was played against Northamptonshire at Middlesbrough. A year later, on 22 April 1978, West Indian paceman Wayne Daniel took seven for 12, playing for Middlesex against Minor Counties at Ipswich, to return the best ever figures in the Benson & Hedges Cup and the first time a bowler took seven wickets in the competition. In 2002 Warwickshire became the last winners of the Benson & Hedges Cup when they beat Essex. It was their second victory, having won in 1994. Essex had also won the trophy twice – in 1979 it was their first cup in any First Class competition.

LEICESTERSHIRE WERE: The FIRST team to score 300 in a Benson & Hedges Cup innings. GEOFF BOYCOTT WAS: The FIRST batsman to score 1,000 runs in Benson & Hedges Cup ties. WAYNE DANIEL WAS: The FIRST bowler to take seven wickets in the Benson & Hedges Cup. WARWICKSHIRE WERE: The LAST winners of the Benson & Hedges Cup

THE FIRST
CENTURY IN A ONE DAY
INTERNATIONAL
D.L. AMISS, ENGLAND V AUSTRALIA AT OLD TRAFFORD, MANCHESTER, LANCASHIRE, ENGLAND. THURSDAY 24 AUGUST 1972.

The second One Day International was the setting for the first ODI century. Australia won the toss, decided to bat and made 222 for eight from their 55 overs. It took England opener Amiss 130 balls to reach his ton and he eventually made 103 as England won by six wickets. The century also earned Amiss the Man of the Match award.

THE FIRST

TEST MATCH AT WHICH

DICKIE BIRD

OFFICIATED AS UMPIRE

ENGLAND V NEW ZEALAND AT HEADINGLEY, ST MICHAEL'S LANE, LEEDS, YORKSHIRE, ENGLAND. THURSDAY 5 JULY 1973.

Regarded by many as the world's best umpire, Harold Dennis 'Dickie' Bird stood at Headingley for the first time in the third Test between England and New Zealand. His opposite number was Charlie Elliott. England, with a score of 419, beat New Zealand (276 and 142) by an innings and one run after 13 minutes and 21 balls of play on the morning of the fifth day. Dickie Bird's second Test was the second Test against West Indies in that summer of two three-Test rubbers.

THE ONLY

NON-STRIKER IN

FIRST CLASS CRICKET

GIVEN OUT HANDLED THE BALL

C.I. DEY, NORTHERN TRANSVAAL V ORANGE FREE STATE AT RAMBLERS CRICKET CLUB GROUND, BLOEMFONTEIN, FREE STATE, SOUTH AFRICA. FRIDAY 25 JANUARY 1974.

In late January 1974 Christopher Dey became the only non-striker in First Class cricket given out handled the ball. Playing for Northern Transvaal against Orange Free State in the SAB Currie Cup at Ramblers Cricket Club Ground, Bloemfontein, Dey had scored 20 when, backing up, he bumped into a fielder and fell over with the ball lodged under his body. While Dey was still lying on the ground, the Orange Free State team appealed and the umpire gave him out.

THE ONLY

TEST BATSMAN REINSTATED AFTER BEING RUN OUT

A.I. KALLICHARRAN, WEST INDIES V ENGLAND AT QUEEN'S PARK OVAL, PORT OF SPAIN, TRINIDAD. SUNDAY 3 FEBRUARY 1974.

Tony Greig ran out Alvin Kallicharran, then on 142 not out, as he and Bernard Julien headed off at close of play. West Indies were 274 for six in the first Test at the Queen's Park Oval in Port of Spain, Trinidad when Julien blocked the final ball of the day. Before umpire Douglas Sang Hue could call time, the batsmen headed for the pavilion and Greig picked up the ball and broke Kallicharran's wicket. Since time had not been called, the umpire raised a finger. When all the players were off the pitch the crowd rioted and laid siege to the pavilion. To save the series, and possibly Grieg's neck, the England team withdrew the appeal and Kallicharran was reinstated, the only time this had happened in Test cricket. The next day Kallicharran took his score to 158. West Indies won the match by seven wickets. The incident did not help Greig's reputation, which would be permanently soured for England fans before the end of the decade. (See 1977, page 172.)

THE FIRST

ENGLAND PLAYER TO SCORE A CENTURY AND TAKE FIVE WICKETS IN AN INNINGS

A.W. GREIG, ENGLAND V WEST INDIES, AT KENSINGTON OVAL, BRIDGETOWN, BARBADOS. SUNDAY 10 MARCH 1974.

In the third Test between England and West Indies fast bowler Andy Roberts made his debut for the Windies, thus becoming the first Antiguan to play Test cricket. It was a match of firsts – Lawrence Rowe became the first West Indian to score a triple century (302) against England and all-rounder Tony Greig became the first England player to score a century and take five wickets in an innings of the same Test. The West Indians made 596, helped by a century from Alvin Kallicharran (119), in a high-scoring match that saw England score 395 (Greig 148, Bernard Julien five for 57) and 277 for seven (Keith Fletcher 129 not out) in the drawn game.

THE LAST
TEST APPEARANCE
BY GARY SOBERS

WEST INDIES V ENGLAND AT QUEEN'S PARK OVAL, PORT OF SPAIN, TRINIDAD. FRIDAY 5 APRIL 1974.

In fact, two Test giants bowed out in this match. West Indians Rohan Kanhai and Gary Sobers both played their last games in the fifth Test against England at Port of Spain, Trinidad. England won the six-day Test by just 26 runs, but on 30 March, the opening day, Sobers became the first West Indian to take 100 wickets when he dismissed Dennis Amiss for 44, caught by Kanhai. Lance Gibbs became the second to achieve the feat when he clean bowled Geoff Boycott for 112 in England's second innings. Boycott had scored 99 in the first innings, failing by just one run to become the first Englishman to score a century in both innings against West Indies. Kanhai scored a disappointing two and seven but he did take a catch as wicketkeeper when Deryck Murray temporarily retired with a cut head.

GARY SOBERS WAS ALSO: The FIRST West Indian to take 100 Test wickets

THE LAST
TEST APPEARANCE
BY COLIN COWDREY

ENGLAND V AUSTRALIA AT MELBOURNE CRICKET GROUND, JOLIMONT, MELBOURNE, VICTORIA, AUSTRALIA. THURSDAY 13 FEBRUARY 1975.

The man with the most appropriate initials in cricket – MCC – made his 114th and last Test appearance for England against Australia at the MCG. Michael Colin Cowdrey had made his first appearance, also against Australia, at Brisbane on 26 November 1954 – 20 years, two months and 18 days earlier. He captained England 27 times between 1959 and 1969, winning eight matches, drawing 15 and losing four. In 1972 Cowdrey was appointed CBE, becoming Sir Colin in 1992 and Baron Cowdrey of Tonbridge in the County of Kent in 1997, only the second cricketer to become a peer.

THE FIRST

LIMITED OVERS WORLD CUP

ENGLAND. SATURDAY 7 JUNE 1975.

West Indies won the first World Cup at Lord's on 21 June 1975 against Australia. It was a close-run thing. Windies, batting first, made 291 for eight from their 60 overs with captain Clive Lloyd scoring 102. Despite the pace of Dennis Lillee, Jeff Thomson and Max Walker, it was Gary Gilmour who was the top wicket-taker, capturing five West Indian scalps for 48. The Australians set off for their target with a vengeance but, whenever they went for a quick single, so it seemed Viv Richards was there to run them out. Five Australians lost their wickets that way, three falling victim to King Viv. Australia were on 233 for nine and victory seemed assured for the Windies, but the last pair, Thomson and Lillee, had other ideas. Needing just 18 runs for victory, at 8.42 pm Thomson was run out by wicketkeeper Deryck Murray to give West Indies the honour of winning the first World Cup.

THE ONLY

PLAYER TO PLAY IN CRICKET AND FOOTBALL WORLD CUPS

I.V.A RICHARDS, ANTIGUA V TRINIDAD AT PORT OF SPAIN, TRINIDAD. FRIDAY 10 NOVEMBER 1972; WEST INDIES V SRI LANKA AT OLD TRAFFORD, MANCHESTER, ENGLAND. SATURDAY 7 JUNE 1975.

Viv Richards represented Antigua in qualifying matches for the 1974 World Cup but the team did not make the finals. Richards did not have much to do in his first cricket World Cup match. West Indies bowled out Sri Lanka for 86 in 37.2 overs and then reached their target of 87 with the loss of one wicket in 20.4 overs. Richards did not bat, bowl or take a catch.

THE ONLY

PLAYER TO APPEAR IN CUP FINALS
AT LORD'S AND WEMBLEY

G.F. Cross, Leicester City v Manchester United at Wembley Stadium, Middlesex, England. Saturday 25 May 1963; Leicestershire v Middlesex at Lord's Cricket Ground, St John's Wood Road, St John's Wood, Middlesex, England. Saturday 19 July 1975.

Graham Cross was a successful cricketer and footballer. He played 599 games for Leicester City – a club record – and appeared in two FA Cup Finals (1963 and 1969) and two League Cup Finals (1964 and 1965) for the Filbert Street club. He won 11 Under-23 caps for England but never made it to the first team. He also played for Chesterfield, Brighton and Hove Albion, Preston North End, Lincoln City, Enderby Town and Hinckley Athletic. Leicester City lost the 1963 FA Cup Final 3-1 to Manchester United and fared no better six years later when they lost 1-0 to the other Mancunian side, Manchester City.

Cross made his debut for Leicestershire in 1961 and played 83 games, scoring 2,079 runs with a top score of 78. He took 92 wickets with a best of four for 28. In 1975 he was on the winning side in the fourth Benson & Hedges Cup as Leicestershire beat Middlesex by five wickets. Cross's contribution was less than impressive – Fred Titmus had him lbw for a duck and with the ball he took nought for nine from two overs.

THE FIRST
STREAKER AT A
TEST MATCH IN ENGLAND

M. ANGELOW AT LORD'S CRICKET GROUND, ST JOHN'S WOOD ROAD, ST JOHN'S WOOD, MIDDLESEX, ENGLAND. MONDAY 4 AUGUST 1975.

Perhaps in an attempt to emulate his namesake's famous sculpture *David*, merchant navy cook Michael Angelow celebrated Michelangelo's quincentenary by stripping down to his trainers and socks, running on to the pitch at Lord's and hurdling both sets of stumps.

Sixteen months earlier Australian stockbroker Michael O'Brien had bet a friend that streaking would catch on in Britain. He then ran on to the pitch during a rugby union international at Twickenham before famously being led away with only a policeman's helmet to preserve his modesty. (PC Bruce Perry later said: 'I felt embarrassed so I covered him up as best I could. It was a cold day – he had nothing to be proud of.') O'Brien was fined by the courts and sacked by his employer, but at least he won his bet: by the end of the decade streaking had spread to several other sports, including cricket.

When Angelow introduced streaking to cricket during the second Test of the 1975 Ashes series reactions were mixed: Greg Chappell was not amused, Alan Turner is said to have roared with laughter, and one commentator simply said: 'Well I've seen nothing like this at Lord's before.' The crowd cheered and journalists had a field day with puns about no balls, googlies, ball tampering and merchant seamen. Even the St John's Wood magistrates saw the funny side, fining Angelow the exact amount that he had won in a bet with his friends (various reports put the size of the bet and the fine at £10, £20 and £25). More than 20 years later Greg Chappell was still not amused, complaining that Angelow had started a fad that demeaned the sport. Angelow, on the other hand, said that he loved cricket and had waited for the end of Dennis Lillee's over so as not to disrupt the game.

------◆◆◆------

THE ONLY
MAN TO PLAY FIRST CLASS
CRICKET AND FIRST CLASS FOOTBALL
ON THE SAME DAY

J.C. BALDERSTONE, LEICESTERSHIRE V DERBYSHIRE AT CHESTERFIELD, DERBYSHIRE, ENGLAND; DONCASTER ROVERS V BRENTFORD AT BELLE VUE, DONCASTER, LINCOLNSHIRE, ENGLAND. MONDAY 15 SEPTEMBER 1975.

Chris Balderstone became the only man to play First Class cricket and first class football on the same day. He played for Leicestershire against Derbyshire at Queen's Park, Chesterfield and was on 51 when bad light stopped play. That evening he turned out in midfield for Doncaster Rovers in a 1-1 draw against Brentford in Division Four. When that match had finished, he played darts for Doncaster Rovers players' team against a supporters' team in the Rovers supporters' club. The following day he resumed his innings and was finally run out for 116. He died aged 59 on 6 March 2000.

THE ONLY
WICKETKEEPER TO EXCEED 1,500 FIRST CLASS DISMISSALS
J.T. MURRAY, MIDDLESEX. 1952–1975.

Middlesex's custodian of the gloves John Murray is the only wicketkeeper to take in excess of 1,500 victims. In 23 years behind the stumps Murray caught 1,268 batsmen and stumped 259 more. John Thomas Murray was born on April Fool's Day 1935 and made his First Class debut on 24 May 1952 at Grace Road, Leicester. He did not bat in the first innings and was out for three in the second. He took one catch. In his career he played 635 First Class matches and scored 18,872 runs with a top score of 142. Between 1961 and 1967 he played 21 Tests for England, hitting 506 runs, with one century (112) to his credit. He lost his place in the side to Alan Knott.

THE ONLY
FATHER AND SON TO SCORE CENTURIES ON TEST DEBUT
L. AMARNATH, INDIA V ENGLAND AT GYMKHANA GROUND, BOMBAY, INDIA. SUNDAY 17 DECEMBER 1933; S. AMARNATH, INDIA V NEW ZEALAND AT EDEN PARK, AUCKLAND, NEW ZEALAND. SUNDAY 25 JANUARY 1976.

In India's first official home Test Lala Amarnath became the first Indian to score a century at home. He made 118 but England won the match by nine wickets. His son, Surinder, hit 124 in the first Test of the 1975–1976 rubber against the Kiwis, sharing a partnership of 204 for the second wicket with Sunil Gavaskar. Surinder Amarnath became the fourth Indian to score a century on his Test debut as India won by eight wickets. Lala Amarnath is also unique in having two sons who have played Test cricket – Mohinder Amarnath made his debut on Christmas Eve 1969 against Australia.

THE FIRST
PLAYER TO BAT IN A HELMET IN A TEST MATCH

D.L. AMISS, ENGLAND V WEST INDIES AT THE OVAL, KENNINGTON, SURREY, ENGLAND. FRIDAY 13 AUGUST 1976.

England opener Dennis Amiss was the first player to wear a helmet in a Test match when he donned the protective headgear against the might of the West Indian pace attack. It certainly helped, as Amiss made 203 before being bowled by Michael Holding, although West Indies won by 231 runs.

THE ONLY
AUSTRALIAN TO SCORE A CENTURY IN EACH INNINGS OF SUCCESSIVE FIRST CLASS MATCHES

D.W. HOOKES, SOUTH AUSTRALIA V QUEENSLAND AT ADELAIDE OVAL, WAR MEMORIAL DRIVE, NORTH ADELAIDE, SOUTH AUSTRALIA, AUSTRALIA. 11 FEBRUARY 1977; SOUTH AUSTRALIA V NEW SOUTH WALES AT ADELAIDE OVAL, WAR MEMORIAL DRIVE, NORTH ADELAIDE, SOUTH AUSTRALIA, AUSTRALIA. 18 FEBRUARY 1977.

Regarded as one of Australia's great batting hopes, David Hookes scored 185 and 107 against Queensland and then followed that up with 135 and 156 against New South Wales, both on his home ground. Hookes finished the season with an average of 71.75. In the Centenary Test he came to public notice when he hit England captain Tony Greig for five consecutive boundaries. However, Hookes never managed to live up to his initial promise. Signing with Kerry Packer's World Series Cricket was a mistake he regretted. Of his career, Hookes said, 'I suspect history will judge me harshly as a batsman because of my modest record in 23 Tests and I can't complain about that.' He died in the evening of 19 January 2004, aged 48, after being punched by hotel bouncer Zdravko Micevic, a former boxer, outside the Beaconsfield Hotel in St Kilda, Melbourne. Hookes had been drinking with Victoria and South Australia players following Victoria's victory in a match the previous day. Hookes fell, hit his head and suffered a heart attack caused by shock. He was taken to Alfred Hospital, Prahran, Melbourne and put on a life-support machine. He died not long after being taken off the machine. On 22 August 2005 Micevic, 23, went on trial accused of Hookes's manslaughter. He was acquitted on 12 September 2005 after the jury deliberated for five days.

THE LAST
ENGLAND MATCH OVERSEAS
AS MCC

MCC V WESTERN AUSTRALIA AT WESTERN AUSTRALIA CRICKET ASSOCIATION GROUND, NELSON CRESCENT, EAST PERTH, PERTH, WESTERN AUSTRALIA, AUSTRALIA. SATURDAY 5 MARCH 1977.

England's last overseas tour match under the colours of the MCC took place at Western Australia Cricket Association Ground, Perth against Western Australia. Apart from Tests, when touring abroad the England team officially played as MCC until the 1976–1977 tour of Australia. Western Australia won the toss and decided to bat. Captained by wicketkeeper Rodney Marsh, they made 326 for eight declared with Craig Serjeant unbeaten on 101. In reply, MCC scored 244 for eight declared, with opening batsman Mike Brearley top scoring on 61. Western Australia declared for a second time on 218 for four and, by the time the match ended on 7 March, MCC were 239 for eight. Bob Woolmer made 51. When he reached 26 he passed the milestone of 7,500 runs in First Class matches. The last time the England touring team wore the 'bacon and egg' colours of MCC was on the 1996–1997 tour of New Zealand.

THE FIRST

TEST MATCH WITH MIKE BREARLEY AS ENGLAND CAPTAIN

ENGLAND V AUSTRALIA AT LORD'S CRICKET GROUND, ST JOHN'S WOOD ROAD, ST JOHN'S WOOD, MIDDLESEX, ENGLAND. THURSDAY 16 JUNE 1977.

Mike Brearley captained England for the first time after Tony Greig's involvement in Kerry Packer's Circus was revealed and Greig was stripped of the captaincy. Brearley led the team out at Lord's in the first Test of the Ashes series. The match – the first of 31 in charge – was drawn but Brearley was on course to become the second most successful England captain of all time (after Douglas Jardine). Brearley won 18, drew nine and lost just four Tests and so achieved a success rate of 77.77 per cent. His batting ability was modest: he averaged 22 and never made a century.

THE FIRST CRICKET MATCH PLAYED ON ASTROTURF

AMERICA V WEST INDIES AT GIANTS STADIUM, 50 ROUTE 120, EAST RUTHERFORD, NEW JERSEY, UNITED STATES OF AMERICA. SUNDAY 4 SEPTEMBER 1977.

America beat West Indies at Giants Stadium in the first match played on Astroturf. Gary Sobers and his Caribbean All-Stars lost an afternoon of gentle cricket, watched by 6,674 people who had paid $50,000. Well, perhaps not so gentle. Instead of discreet applause, tea, and the sound of leather on willow the crowd was treated to an electronic scoreboard that flashed up messages like 'Give that man a hand!', 'Did you see that?' and 'Boing!' Giants Stadium was demolished in 2010.

THE FIRST
WORLD SERIES CRICKET
'SUPERTEST'

WSC AUSTRALIA V WSC WEST INDIES AT VFL PARK, 2 STADIUM
CIRCUIT, MULGRAVE MELBOURNE, VICTORIA, AUSTRALIA. FRIDAY
2 DECEMBER 1977.

Denied the right to broadcast Test cricket in Australia, media mogul Kerry Packer set up his own World Series Cricket on 6 April 1977.

The first 'Supertest' was between WSC Australia and WSC West Indies. The tourists won the toss and elected to field. WSC Australia made 256 in their first innings with the top score coming from spin bowler Ray Bright with 69. Opener Rick McCosker, Greg Chappell and great white hope David Hookes all went for a duck. Michael Holding took four for 60. WSC West Indies hit 214 with Viv Richards hitting 79 and the WSC Windies' wickets being spread between Dennis Lillee, Len Pascoe, Max Walker, Hookes and Bright. WSC Australia made 192 in their second knock with 110 of the runs coming from McCosker (47) and Hookes (63). Andy Roberts was the most successful WSC Windies bowler with four for 52. The target to reach was 235 and WSC West Indies won by three wickets when they achieved 237 for seven.

The first 'Supertest' between WSC Australia and WSC World XI began at Sydney on 14 January 1978. WSC Australia batted first and scored 304 off 82.7 eight-ball overs. Bruce Laird scored 106 but the next highest scorer was captain Ian Chappell, way behind on 44. Springbok Mike Proctor, who was unable to play Test cricket because of apartheid, took four for 33 and West Indian Joel Garner returned figures of three for 71. In their first innings WSC World XI hit 290 with a century from Viv Richards and 57 from Barry Richards, another South African denied international cricket. Max Walker took seven for 88 and Gary Gilmour picked up the other three wickets at a cost of 103. WSC Australia collapsed in the second innings and were all out for 128 with Martin Kent, one of the few non-international players signed by Packer, scoring 31. WSC World XI needed 143 to win and achieved the target with the loss of six wickets. The match, originally intended to last for five days, was extended to six to ensure a result.

THE FIRST
FLOODLIT MATCH
WSC AUSTRALIA V WSC WORLD XI AT VFL PARK, 2 STADIUM CIRCUIT,
MULGRAVE MELBOURNE, VICTORIA, AUSTRALIA. WEDNESDAY
14 DECEMBER 1977.

The first cricket match to be played under floodlights was WSC Australia against WSC World XI at VFL Park, Melbourne. The lights were switched on at 6.30 pm and a red ball was exchanged for a white one, after orange and yellow balls were found to be unsuitable. The sightscreens were turned around and were painted black and bouncers were banned. WSC Australia won the toss and decided to field. WSC World XI made 207. In reply, WSC Australia made 210 for four with the Chappell brothers making the runs – Ian with 69 and Greg, who was Man of the Match, made 59. Derek Underwood took all four wickets as WSC Australia won by six wickets.

THE LAST
DELIVERY OF AN EIGHT-BALL OVER
IN AUSTRALIAN NON-TEST CRICKET
T.M. ALDERMAN, WESTERN AUSTRALIA V SOUTH AUSTRALIA AT WESTERN AUSTRALIA
CRICKET ASSOCIATION GROUND, NELSON CRESCENT, EAST PERTH, PERTH, WESTERN
AUSTRALIA, AUSTRALIA. MONDAY 5 MARCH 1979.

Terry Alderman bowled the last ball in the last Sheffield Shield match to feature eight-ball overs at Western Australia Cricket Association Ground, Perth in a game between Western Australia and South Australia. Western Australia won the toss and decided to field. South Australia were bowled out for 107 with Bruce Yardley taking five for 27. Western Australia made 293 with Tony Mann making 84. Alderman took six South Australia wickets for 63 as Western Australia won by an innings and 41 runs. After this match two Tests were played between Australia and Pakistan and the Pakistani tourists met South Australia in a warm-up game.

THE LAST
DELIVERY IN THE LAST
EIGHT-BALL OVER IN
AUSTRALIAN FIRST CLASS CRICKET

MUDASSAR NAZAR, PAKISTAN V AUSTRALIA AT WESTERN AUSTRALIA CRICKET ASSOCIATION GROUND, NELSON CRESCENT, EAST PERTH, PERTH, WESTERN AUSTRALIA, AUSTRALIA. THURSDAY 29 MARCH 1979.

With the change of Law 22 in 2000, eight-ball overs were outlawed the world over but until 1978–1979 they were still used in matches in Australia and New Zealand. Coincidentally, the last ball of an eight-ball over in both Sheffield Shield and Test cricket occurred at the WACA in Perth. Australia won the toss and decided to field. Pakistan made 277 with Javed Miandad the top scorer on 129 not out. Alan Hurst took four for 61. In their first knock Australia made 327. In their second innings Pakistan scored 285 all out with Hurst taking four for 94. Australia were set a target of 236 and after a few stumbles – Rick Darling and Bruce Yardley were run out and opener Andrew Hilditch was out handled the ball (the first Test batsman to be given out in that fashion in Australian First Class cricket) – they made 236 for three to win by seven wickets. Medium pace bowler Mudassar Nazar delivered the last ball of the last eight-ball over in Australia.

THIS MATCH INCLUDED: The FIRST Test batsman to be given out handled the ball in Australian First Class cricket

━◆◆◆◆━

THE LAST
WORLD SERIES CRICKET
'SUPERTEST'

WSC West Indies v WSC Australia at Antigua Recreation Ground, St John's, Antigua. Tuesday 10 April 1979.

The last 'Supertest' between WSC Australia and WSC West Indies ended in a draw at Antigua Recreation Ground, St John's, Antigua. WSC West Indies won the toss and chose to field. They dismissed the WSC tourists for 234. Greg Chappell made a century but seven players failed to get to double figures (Bruce Laird two, David Hookes two, Rodney Marsh nought, Ray Bright nought, Dennis Lillee six, Jeff Thomson four, Len Pascoe eight not out). Colin Croft took four for 56 and Andy Roberts four for 73. WSC West Indies made 438, with Laurence Rowe top scoring with 135 and Lillee took six wickets for 125. When the match ended Australia were on 415 for six with wicketkeeper Marsh unbeaten on 102. A fortnight later, on 24 April, the Australian Cricket Board gave Kerry Packer exclusive rights to show matches organized by them for ten years.

THE ONLY
BOWLER TO TAKE AN LBW HAT-TRICK
TWICE IN
FIRST CLASS CRICKET

M.J. PROCTER, GLOUCESTERSHIRE V ESSEX AT CHALKWELL PARK, THE RIDGEWAY, WESTCLIFF-ON-SEA, ESSEX, ENGLAND. TUESDAY 18 JULY 1972; GLOUCESTERSHIRE V YORKSHIRE AT COLLEGE SPORTS GROUND, THIRLESTAINE ROAD, CHELTENHAM, GLOUCESTERSHIRE, ENGLAND. TUESDAY 14 AUGUST 1979.

Wisden Cricketer of the Year in 1970, fast bowler Mike Procter took a hat-trick of wickets lbw in Essex's second innings as Gloucestershire won by 107 runs at Westcliff-on-Sea, Essex. Procter took five for 30, including the wickets of Graham Saville, Brian Ward and Keith Boyce, to leave Essex at one stage 17 for four. Seven years later Procter, by then county captain, repeated his achievement in a match limited to 100 overs per first innings. Procter took six for 107 and in his lbw hat-trick captured the wickets of Richard Lumb, Bill Athey and his opposing captain John Hampshire.

THE ONLY
ALUMINIUM BAT
IN TEST CRICKET

D.K. LILLEE, AUSTRALIA V ENGLAND AT WESTERN AUSTRALIA CRICKET
ASSOCIATION GROUND, NELSON CRESCENT, EAST PERTH, PERTH, WESTERN
AUSTRALIA, AUSTRALIA. TUESDAY 18 DECEMBER 1979.

Australian fast bowler Dennis Lillee threw a tantrum and an aluminium
bat 'fully 40 yards towards the pavilion' after England captain Mike
Brearley complained about its use on the fourth day of the first Test at the
WACA Cricket Ground in Perth. Lillee employed the bat as a publicity
stunt for a friend's company and had used it previously against West Indies
without incident. However, after Lillee had hit three, Brearley told the
umpires that he believed the ball had been damaged. Australian captain
Greg Chappell sent out 12th man Rodney Hogg with a traditional willow
bat, but Lillee refused to change bats until Chappell himself came out and
insisted. Lillee eventually scored 19 before Peter Willey caught him off
Graham Dilley and Australia won the Test, which was not an Ashes
match, by 138 runs. In 1980 the Laws of the game were changed to outlaw
bats not made of wood.

THE ONLY
TEST MATCH INTERRUPTED
BY A SOLAR ECLIPSE

INDIA V ENGLAND AT WANKHEDE STADIUM, BOMBAY, INDIA. SATURDAY
16 FEBRUARY 1980.

The rest day of the Jubilee Test between India and England was brought
forward a day because astronomers predicted an 87 per cent solar eclipse
on the afternoon of the second day. Neither the Indian cricket board nor
the England team management wanted the responsibility of the 50,000

fans potentially going blind by staring at the solar eclipse. It was all in vain – as Bob Willis recalled, 'It was an anticlimax. The sky only slightly darkened mid-afternoon.'

THE FIRST
PLAYER TO SCORE A CENTURY
AND TAKE TEN WICKETS
IN A TEST MATCH
I.T. BOTHAM, ENGLAND V INDIA AT WANKHEDE STADIUM, BOMBAY, INDIA. TUESDAY 19 FEBRUARY 1980.

England all-rounder Ian Botham became the first man to score a century and take ten wickets in a Test match when he scored 114 and took six for 58 and seven for 48 in the Golden Jubilee Test against India at Wankhede Stadium, Bombay. No other player in the match scored a half-century as England won by ten wickets more than a day and a half ahead of schedule.

THE ONLY
PLAYER TO HIT
150 IN BOTH INNINGS
OF A TEST MATCH
A.R. BORDER, AUSTRALIA V PAKISTAN AT GADDAFI STADIUM, LAHORE, PAKISTAN. SUNDAY 23 MARCH 1980.

Allan Border of Australia became the only batsman to score 150 or more in both innings of a Test match when, having scored 153 at Gaddafi Stadium, Lahore in the second innings of the third Test, he was stumped by captain and stand-in wicketkeeper Javed Miandad. In the first innings he was 150 not out in the match, which ended in a draw. The match was also unusual in that, in Australia's first innings, Pakistan used nine bowlers (all but wicketkeeper Taslim Arif and Azmat Rana) and used ten bowlers in the second knock (everyone except Azmat Rana).

THE LAST
FAMILY WITH THREE
GENERATIONS
OF FIRST CLASS CRICKETERS

J.H. PARKS,
SUSSEX V SURREY AT THE OVAL, KENNINGTON, SURREY, ENGLAND.
WEDNESDAY 4 JUNE 1924;

J.M. PARKS,
SUSSEX V CAMBRIDGE UNIVERSITY AT CRICKETFIELD ROAD,
HORSHAM, SUSSEX, ENGLAND. SATURDAY 11 JUNE 1949;

R.J. PARKS,
HAMPSHIRE V SUSSEX AT COUNTY GROUND, NORTHLANDS
ROAD, SOUTHAMPTON, HAMPSHIRE, ENGLAND.
WEDNESDAY 4 JUNE 1980.

The last family to date to supply three generations of First Class cricketers is the Parks. Grandfather Jim made his debut at The Oval, scored an unbeaten 17 in his only innings (batting at number 11) and took a catch as the match ended in a draw. In a career that lasted until 1952 he played in 468 First Class matches, scoring 21,369 runs with a top score of 197. His son, also Jim, outdid his father, playing as wicketkeeper in 46 Tests compared to his dad's one. He was also a *Wisden* Cricketer of the Year in 1968, the second year he captained Sussex. Between 1954 and 1967–1968 he played 739 First Class matches, scoring 36,673 runs with a top score of an unbeaten 205. In his first match he scored 12 and one not out and took one wicket for nine runs. His son Bobby kept wicket for Hampshire but lacked the talent of his father and grandfather. The closest he got to playing for England was at Lord's in 1986 when wicketkeeper Bruce French was hit by a Richard Hadlee bouncer and Parks was called in on his day off. (See 1937, page 121).

The Cowdreys are likely to be the first family to supply four generations of First Class cricketers: great-grandfather Ernest, grandfather Colin, father Chris and son Fabian.

THE ONLY
PLAYER TO HIT A SIX ON ALL FIVE DAYS OF A TEST MATCH
K.J. HUGHES, AUSTRALIA V ENGLAND AT LORD'S CRICKET GROUND, ST JOHN'S WOOD ROAD, ST JOHN'S WOOD, MIDDLESEX, ENGLAND. THURSDAY 28 AUGUST 1980.

Hughes achieved the feat in the 1980 Centenary Test, the 885th Test match played and the 240th between the two countries. It ended in a draw. Hughes is one of five players, and the only Australian, to have batted on all five days of a Test. Geoff Boycott and Allan Lamb are the two English players to have batted every day. The other two are Ravi Shastri and Motganhalli Jaisimha, both of India.

THE LAST
GILLETTE CUP FINAL
MIDDLESEX V KENT AT LORD'S CRICKET GROUND, ST JOHN'S WOOD ROAD, ST JOHN'S WOOD, MIDDLESEX, ENGLAND. SATURDAY 6 SEPTEMBER 1980.

The last Gillette Cup Final was held at Lord's and Middlesex beat Kent by seven wickets. Man of the Match was Middlesex captain Mike Brearley who scored 96 not out. From 1981 the competition was known as the NatWest Trophy.

THE LAST
UNDERARM BOWLING IN A LIMITED OVERS INTERNATIONAL
T.M. Chappell, Australia v New Zealand at Melbourne Cricket Ground, Jolimont, Melbourne, Victoria, Australia. Sunday 1 February 1981.

The last underarm delivery in a limited overs international was the last ball of the last over of a match between Australia and New Zealand – and it was considered so underhand that the practice was banned in Australia the following week.

It was the third 50-over match of a best-of-five World Cup Series, Australia and New Zealand having won a game apiece. Australia batted first and made 235 for four. New Zealand replied with 221 for six in 49 overs, leaving them with a target of 15 runs from the final over to win. Trevor Chappell had the responsibility of not conceding those 15 runs, and it must have been with some trepidation that he stepped up to bowl the final over.

Richard Hadlee hit the first ball for four, leaving 11 runs required. Chappell bowled Hadlee with the second ball. Ian Smith hit the third and fourth balls for two each. Seven runs were now required. Chappell bowled Smith with the fifth ball. New Zealand batsman Brian McKechnie came in, knowing that he must score six off the final ball to tie the game which, under World Series rules, would have forced a replay. It was an unlikely scenario but Aussie captain Greg Chappell knew that McKechnie, an All Black as well as a cricketer, had the power to do it. So Greg Chappell instructed his younger brother to bowl the last ball underarm, thus making it impossible for McKechnie to hit a six.

After discussing the legality with the umpires (underarm deliveries were already outlawed in English one-day games), Trevor did as Greg had ordered – to the disgust of the crowd, the batsman, the New Zealand Prime Minister, the Australian Cricket Board and most of the cricketing world. Even Greg Chappell later conceded that his decision was a mistake. The ball rolled along the wicket and all McKechnie could do was to block it – and then throw down his bat in protest. New Zealand Prime Minister Robert Muldoon described Chappell's decision as an act of cowardice appropriate to a team playing in yellow. The Australian Cricket Board did not attempt to refute Muldoon's accusation, and issued a statement saying:

'The Board deplores Greg Chappell's action and has advised him of the Board's strong feelings on this matter and of his responsibilities as Australia's captain to uphold the spirit of the game at all times.

We acknowledge that his action was within the Laws of the game, but it was totally contrary to the spirit in which cricket has been, and should be, played.'

A few days later Australia won the fourth game and Greg Chappell was voted Man of the World Series.

THE LAST

TEST APPEARANCE
BY GEOFF BOYCOTT
ENGLAND v INDIA

AT EDEN GARDENS, CALCUTTA, INDIA. WEDNESDAY 6 JANUARY 1982.

Geoff Boycott left the Test cricket arena for the 108th and last time in 1982. In an international career that had started on 4 June 1964 and lasted 17 years, seven months and two days Boycott hit 20 centuries and 42 half-centuries among 8,114 runs, over 193 innings, with a top score of 246 not out and an average of 47.72. In his last match, played at Eden Gardens, Calcutta, opening the batting with Graham Gooch, he scored a disappointing 18 and six.

THE FIRST

TEST MATCH FOR
SRI LANKA

SRI LANKA V ENGLAND AT PAIKIASOTHY SARAVANAMUTTU STADIUM, COLOMBO, SRI LANKA. WEDNESDAY 17 FEBRUARY 1982.

Sri Lanka were admitted to full membership of the ICC on 21 July 1981 becoming the eighth Test-playing nation. They played their first Test match against England in February 1982. Sri Lanka won the toss and decided to bat. They were bowled out by England for 218, Ranjan Madugalle hitting 65 and Arjuna Ranatunga 54. Spinner Derek Underwood took five for 28. England then made just five more with David Gower the top scorer on 89. In their second knock the Sri Lankans made 175 and John Emburey took six for 33. England reached their target with ease, scoring 171 for three to win by seven wickets.

THE FIRST

'REBEL TEST'
MATCH IN SOUTH AFRICA

South Africa v South African Breweries English XI at New Wanderers Stadium, Johannesburg, Gauteng, South Africa. Friday 12 March 1982.

After 12 years in the cricketing wilderness because of apartheid, South Africa hired a number of English Test players, past and present, to play a series of unofficial 'Tests'. The first unofficial 'Test' saw South Africa play SA English XI, captained by Graham Gooch and including Geoff Boycott, Wayne Larkins, Dennis Amiss, Bob Woolmer, Peter Willey, Derek Underwood, Alan Knott, Chris Old and John Lever. South Africa won the toss, decided to bat and made 400 for seven declared. Jimmy Cook scored 114 and Peter Kirsten 84. In reply, SAB English XI were bowled out for 150 with Amiss hitting an undefeated 66 and captain Gooch scoring 30. Top Springbok bowler was pace man Vintcent van der Bijl who took five for 25. Following on, SAB English XI were all out for 283 with van der Bijl taking five for 79. Apart from Gooch, who scored 109, no other player made more than 36. South Africa easily made their target and, at 37 for two, won by eight wickets. A week later, Gooch was banned from playing Test cricket for three years for his participation in the tour.

THE FIRST

WICKETKEEPER TO SCORE 3,000 RUNS
AND MAKE 300 DISMISSALS IN TESTS

R.W. MARSH, AUSTRALIA V NEW ZEALAND AT LANCASTER PARK, CHRISTCHURCH, NEW ZEALAND. SATURDAY 20 MARCH 1982.

Australia's moustachioed guardian of the stumps Rodney Marsh is the only wicketkeeper to score 3,000 runs and make 300 dismissals in Test matches – an achievement that came about when he caught Martin Crowe off Dennis Lillee in 1982, the 88th time that configuration had appeared on the scorecard.

THE ONLY
FIRST CLASS PLAYER
TO SCORE A CENTURY IN BOTH INNINGS
WITH A RUNNER

G. FOWLER, LANCASHIRE V WARWICKSHIRE AT TRAFALGAR ROAD GROUND, SOUTHPORT, MERSEYSIDE, ENGLAND. WEDNESDAY 28 JULY 1982.

Warwickshire won the toss and decided to bat, which turned out to be a good decision, as they made 523 for four declared with double centuries from both West Indian Alvin Kallicharran and wicketkeeper Geoff Humpage. While fielding Graeme Fowler pulled a thigh muscle and, although he was able to bat on the first day, his injury worsened over night and he had to resort to using a runner. Warwickshire collapsed to 111 all out in their second innings, leaving Lancashire a modest target to aim for which they made without losing any wickets, with Fowler scoring 128. When Fowler completed his second ton, a fielder came forward to shake hands with the runner who raised his bat in acknowledgement of cheers from the crowd.

THE ONLY
TEST BATSMAN TO RETIRE NOT OUT

C.G. GREENIDGE, WEST INDIES V INDIA AT ANTIGUA RECREATION GROUND, ST JOHN'S, ANTIGUA, WEST INDIES. SATURDAY 30 APRIL 1983.

West Indies opener Gordon Greenidge was the only man in Test history to retire not out. Playing in the fifth Test against India at Antigua Recreation Ground, St John's, Greenidge and Desmond Haynes put on 296 for the first wicket before Ravi Shastri caught Haynes for 136 off the bowling of Yashpal Sharma. Fast bowler Winston Davis came in as nightwatchman and stumps were drawn when he was on one not out and the score 301 for one. Greenidge's daughter was gravely ill in hospital and he abandoned the match to be with her. She died two days later and he was made Man of the Match.

THE ONLY

BOWLER TO TAKE
ALL TEN WICKETS IN A
WEST INDIES FIRST CLASS MATCH

E.E. HEMMINGS, INTERNATIONAL XI V WEST INDIES XI AT SABINA PARK,
KINGSTON, JAMAICA, WEST INDIES. TUESDAY 27 SEPTEMBER 1983.

Spinner Eddie Hemmings became the only bowler to take all ten wickets
in a First Class match in the West Indies when he took ten for 175 while
playing for an International XI against West Indies XI at Sabina Park,
Kingston in the Shell/Air Florida Cricket Festival. The West Indies XI
made 419 and Hemmings's was the most expensive ten wicket bowling
analysis in First Class cricket.

THE FIRST

BATSMAN TO SCORE A CENTURY
IN FIRST AND LAST TESTS

**G.S. CHAPPELL, AUSTRALIA V PAKISTAN AT SYDNEY CRICKET
GROUND, MOORE PARK, MOORE PARK ROAD, SYDNEY, NEW SOUTH
WALES, AUSTRALIA. FRIDAY 6 JANUARY 1984.**

Greg Chappell played his 87th and last Test match for Australia in 1984.
He made his Test debut against England at Perth in 1970–1971 and his
last match was against Pakistan. He became the first player to score a ton

---

TWO TONS

On 6 March 2000 Mohammad Azharuddin played in his 99th and last Test
(before allegations of match-fixing ended his international career) and
became the second batsman to score a century in both his first and last Test
matches. He scored 110 in his first match against England at Calcutta and
102 against South Africa at Bangalore. (See 1985, page 188.)

in both his first and last Tests – hitting 108 in the first and 182 in his last. He was named Man of the Match in his last match.

THE LAST
TEST APPEARANCE BY RODNEY MARSH

R.W. MARSH, AUSTRALIA V PAKISTAN AT SYDNEY CRICKET GROUND, MOORE PARK, MOORE PARK ROAD, SYDNEY, NEW SOUTH WALES, AUSTRALIA. FRIDAY 6 JANUARY 1984.

Australian wicketkeeping legend Rodney Marsh hung up his gloves for the last time after taking 343 catches and 12 stumpings in 96 Tests. The words 'caught Marsh bowled Lillee' were recorded an incredible 95 times in Test scorecards. The moustachioed Marsh would have undoubtedly played a hundred or more Tests for his country had he not signed for Kerry Packer's World Series Cricket Circus. Remarkably, for such a devoted servant to Australia, from May 2003 until June 2005 Marsh was an England selector. On his appointment he said, 'If I'm still a selector when England next play Australia [in 2005] then I'll be rooting for England to win.'

THE FIRST
HINDU TO REPRESENT PAKISTAN IN A TEST MATCH

ANIL DALPAT, PAKISTAN V ENGLAND AT NATIONAL STADIUM, KARACHI, PAKISTAN. FRIDAY 2 MARCH 1984.

Wicketkeeper Anil Dalpat became the first Hindu to play Test cricket for Pakistan. Playing against England at National Stadium, Karachi, he scored 12 and 16 not out and took one catch (to dismiss Allan Lamb). His Test career was quite brief, lasting just nine matches.

THE ONLY

TEST PLAYER
TO OPEN THE INNINGS
AND NEVER BE OUT

T.A. LLOYD, ENGLAND V WEST INDIES, AT EDGBASTON, EDGBASTON ROAD, EDGBASTON, BIRMINGHAM, WEST MIDLANDS, ENGLAND. THURSDAY 14 JUNE 1984.

Andy Lloyd made his Test debut for England against West Indies at Edgbaston, his home ground. Lloyd had done well in the One Day Internationals and was expected to replicate his form in the Test arena. Unfortunately, after he had scored ten and been in the middle for 33 minutes with the score on 20 for nought, Windies quick bowler Malcolm Marshall delivered a nasty ball that hit Lloyd on the temple of his helmet. Forced to retire hurt, he spent the rest of the match in hospital with blurred vision. He was unable to play again that year and was never selected for another international, making him the only Test player to open the innings and never be out.

ANDY LLOYD WAS ALSO: The FIRST Shropshire-born player to represent England in a home Test

THE LAST
TEST APPEARANCE
BY CLIVE LLOYD

C.H. LLOYD, WEST INDIES V AUSTRALIA AT SYDNEY CRICKET GROUND, MOORE PARK, MOORE PARK ROAD, SYDNEY, NEW SOUTH WALES, AUSTRALIA. WEDNESDAY 2 JANUARY 1985.

Clive Lloyd, 6 foot 5 inches (1.98 m) tall, made his First Class debut for British Guiana as a left-hand middle order batsman in 1963–1964. He made his debut for Lancashire in 1968, two years after he made his Test debut for West Indies against India at Bombay. A *Wisden* Cricketer of the Year in 1971, he captained West Indies to victory in the first World Cup in 1975. He was criticized as captain for having his fast bowlers intimidate batsmen and for slow over rates, but his success could not be denied. On 28 April 1984 Lloyd became the first West Indian to play 100 Tests in what was also the 100th Test to be played in the Caribbean. Australia won the last match Lloyd played as captain by an innings and 55 runs but he had the last laugh, winning the series by three Tests to one.

THE ONLY
PLAYER TO SCORE A CENTURY IN HIS FIRST THREE TESTS

M. AZHARUDDIN, INDIA V ENGLAND AT EDEN GARDENS, CALCUTTA, INDIA. MONDAY 31 DECEMBER 1984; INDIA V ENGLAND AT M.A. CHIDAMBARAM STADIUM, CHEPAUK, MADRAS, INDIA. SUNDAY 13 JANUARY 1985; INDIA V ENGLAND AT GREEN PARK, KANPUR, INDIA. THURSDAY 31 JANUARY 1985.

Mohammad Azharuddin was born on 8 February 1963 at Hyderabad, India and attended the local Catholic boys' school. He made his Test debut against England during the rubber that England won after going one down. He batted at number five in the third Test at Calcutta and scored 110, before captain David Gower caught him off the bowling of Norman Cowans. In the fourth Test, played at Madras, Azharuddin scored 105 in India's second innings. In the final Test of the rubber at Kanpur, Azharuddin was promoted up the batting order and went in at number three. He scored 122 and 54 not out (scored in just 38 balls).

In 1991 he was named a *Wisden* Cricketer of the Year. Unsurprisingly, he was appointed India's captain and won 14 Tests and 103 ODI matches. He played in 99 Tests and would have joined the century club had he not been involved in match-fixing. Crooked South African captain Hansie Cronje said that it was Azharuddin who introduced him to the bookies that were to ruin his career. The Central Bureau of Investigation's report found the evidence against Azharuddin compelling:

It is clear that Mohammad Azharuddin contributed substantially towards the expanding bookie/player nexus in Indian cricket. The enquiry

---

A CAREER IN POLITICS

It is not just British politics that attracts chancers. On 19 February 2009 Azharuddin became a member of the Indian National Congress party and in the spring of that year he was elected a member of the Lok Sabha, sitting for the Moradabad constituency of Uttar Pradesh.

---

has disclosed that he received large sums of money from the betting syndicates to fix matches. There is also evidence, which discloses that he roped in other players also to fix matches, which resulted in this malaise making further inroads into Indian cricket.

'*The evidence against Azharuddin... clearly establishes that he took money from bookies/punters to fix cricket matches and also the fact that the underworld had approached him to fix matches for them.*'

Azharuddin confessed to fixing three ODI matches and the Board of Control for Cricket in India banned him for life in 2000. Six years later the ban was rescinded, but the ICC insisted that the prohibition should remain in force.

◆━✦━◆

THE FIRST
TEST WIN BY
SRI LANKA

SRI LANKA V INDIA AT PAIKIASOTHY SARAVANAMUTTU STADIUM, COLOMBO, SRI LANKA. WEDNESDAY 11 SEPTEMBER 1985.

Sri Lanka won the toss, decided to bat and made 385 all out. Wicketkeeper and opening batsman Amal Silva scored 111 and Roy Dias 95, while Chetan Sharma took five for 118. In their innings India made 244. Sri Lanka declared their second innings at 206 for three and then bowled out India for 198, with Rumesh Ratnayake taking five Indian wickets for 49. Sri Lanka won by 149 runs, resulting in national celebrations and a public holiday the following day.

THE ONLY

ENGLISH BOWLER
CALLED FOR THROWING
IN A TEST IN
ENGLAND

D.I. GOWER, ENGLAND V NEW ZEALAND AT TRENT BRIDGE, NOTTINGHAM,
NOTTINGHAMSHIRE, ENGLAND. TUESDAY 12 AUGUST 1986.

With the scores level, England captain Mike Gatting gave the ball to
David Gower to bowl the final over. Gower deliberately chucked his only
ball of the match. Technically the game ended with that call but the
Secretary of the TCCB Donald Carr subsequently ruled that the boundary
struck off that ball by Martin Crowe should stand. Gower is thus the only
English bowler called for throwing in a Test match in England.

THE FIRST

PLAYER TO SCORE
10,000 TEST RUNS

S.M. GAVASKAR, INDIA V PAKISTAN AT GUJARAT STADIUM, MOTERA,
AHMEDABAD, INDIA. SATURDAY 7 MARCH 1987.

India's opening batsman Sunil Gavaskar became the first cricketer to score
10,000 runs in Test cricket not long after tea in the fourth Test against
Pakistan at Gujarat Stadium. He achieved the feat when he hit the ball
for a two to take his score to 58. His achievement was greeted by a crowd
invasion that lasted for 20 minutes and that obviously disturbed his
concentration because, in his penultimate Test, he only added five more
runs before Imran Khan had him leg before.

THE FIRST
PLAYER TO SCORE A CENTURY AND TAKE FIVE WICKETS IN AN ODI

I.V.A. RICHARDS, WEST INDIES V NEW ZEALAND AT CARISBROOK, DUNEDIN, NEW ZEALAND. WEDNESDAY 18 MARCH 1987.

West Indies captain Viv Richards was the first player to score a century and take five wickets in a One Day International. In the first One Day International in the Rothmans Cup, New Zealand won the toss and put the tourists into bat. West Indies scored 237 for nine off their 50 overs, with Richards hitting 119. New Zealand were dismissed for 142 with King Viv taking five for 41 as the Windies won by 95 runs. The feat would not be repeated until 21 June 2005 when Paul Collingwood scored 112 not out and took six for 31 against Bangladesh.

THE FIRST
BATSMAN TO SCORE 7,000 RUNS IN JOHN PLAYER LEAGUE MATCHES

D.L. AMISS, WARWICKSHIRE V WORCESTERSHIRE AT WORCESTER, WORCESTERSHIRE, ENGLAND. SUNDAY 5 JULY 1987.

Beginning in 1969, the John Player League – showcasing county stars in 40-over matches, usually beginning about 1 pm on a Sunday afternoon – was responsible for many young people becoming cricket fans. Warwickshire's Dennis Amiss was the first batsman to score 7,000 runs in John Player League matches. He achieved the feat in his 237th innings in a match against Worcestershire.

THE ONLY
CRICKETER TO PLAY
HIS FIRST FOUR TESTS AGAINST
FOUR DIFFERENT COUNTRIES
A.I.C. DODEMAIDE,

AUSTRALIA V NEW ZEALAND AT MELBOURNE CRICKET GROUND, JOLIMONT, MELBOURNE, VICTORIA, AUSTRALIA. SATURDAY 26 DECEMBER 1987;

AUSTRALIA V ENGLAND AT SYDNEY CRICKET GROUND, MOORE PARK, MOORE PARK ROAD, SYDNEY, NEW SOUTH WALES, AUSTRALIA. FRIDAY 29 JANUARY 1988;

AUSTRALIA V SRI LANKA AT WESTERN AUSTRALIA CRICKET ASSOCIATION GROUND, NELSON CRESCENT, EAST PERTH, PERTH, WESTERN AUSTRALIA, AUSTRALIA. FRIDAY 12 FEBRUARY 1988;

AUSTRALIA V PAKISTAN AT NATIONAL STADIUM, KARACHI, PAKISTAN. THURSDAY 15 SEPTEMBER 1988.

Australian pace man Tony Dodemaide took five for 21 on his One Day International debut, against Sri Lanka at Perth in 1987–1988. This was the first instance of anyone taking five wickets in their inaugural ODI match. That same winter he made his Test debut against New Zealand at Melbourne, scored a half-century and took six for 58. Uniquely, he played his first four Tests against four different countries: New Zealand, England, Sri Lanka and Pakistan.

THE ONLY
BOWLER TO TAKE A TEST
HAT-TRICK
WITH BALLS IN THREE SEPARATE OVERS

M.G. HUGHES, AUSTRALIA V WEST INDIES AT WESTERN AUSTRALIA CRICKET ASSOCIATION GROUND, NELSON CRESCENT, EAST PERTH, PERTH, WESTERN AUSTRALIA, AUSTRALIA. SUNDAY 4 DECEMBER 1988.

Australian fast bowler Merv Hughes completed a complicated hat-trick against West Indies at the WACA at Perth. On 3 December, at the end of his 36th over, Hughes had Curtly Ambrose caught by wicketkeeper Ian Healey. At the beginning of his 37th over, he had Patrick Patterson caught by Tony Dodemaide and that completed the Windies' innings.

When he opened the Aussie bowling for the second innings he had Gordon Greenidge out lbw the first ball. Hughes's figures for the match were five for 130 and eight for 87, making 13 for 217 in total.

THE FIRST
BOWLER TO TAKE 400 TEST WICKETS

R.J. HADLEE, NEW ZEALAND V INDIA AT LANCASTER PARK, CHRISTCHURCH, NEW ZEALAND. SUNDAY 4 FEBRUARY 1990.

New Zealand pace man Richard Hadlee dismissed Sanjay Manjrekar to become the first bowler to take 400 wickets in Test cricket. He achieved the feat, which took him 80 Tests, on his home ground of Lancaster Park, Christchurch, when he was 38 years old. Later that summer he was knighted in the Queen's Birthday Honours' List.

THE ONLY
NOBEL PRIZE-WINNER
MENTIONED IN WISDEN

S.B. Beckett, April 1990.

Playwright Samuel Beckett died in Paris, France, aged 83, on 22 December 1989. In 1925 and 1926 he played two First Class games for Dublin University against Northamptonshire. He amassed 35 runs in his four

---

SID ADAMS

On 24 March 1945 spin bowler Sid Adams was killed, aged 40, while crossing the Rhine with the Allies. Leg spinner Adams had taken two wickets with his first two balls in First Class cricket, playing for Northamptonshire against Dublin University in 1926. His first wicket was that of Samuel Beckett.

---

innings as a left-hand opening batsman and, with the ball, he conceded 64 runs without taking a wicket. He won the Nobel Prize in Literature in 1969.

THE FIRST
BROTHERS TO SCORE DOUBLE CENTURIES
IN THE SAME INNINGS
M.E. AND S.R. WAUGH, NEW SOUTH WALES V WESTERN AUSTRALIA AT WESTERN AUSTRALIA CRICKET ASSOCIATION GROUND, NELSON CRESCENT, EAST PERTH, PERTH, WESTERN AUSTRALIA, AUSTRALIA. FRIDAY 21 DECEMBER 1990.

Twins Mark and Steve Waugh shared an unbroken fifth wicket partnership of 464 for their state against Western Australia at Perth. It was the highest ever partnership in First Class cricket in Australia – Mark Waugh was unbeaten on 229 and Steve Waugh not out on 216. It was the first occasion on which brothers scored double centuries in the same innings.

THE FIRST
TWINS TO APPEAR IN THE SAME TEST SIDE
M.E. and S.R. Waugh, Australia v West Indies at Queen's Park Oval, Port of Spain, Trinidad. Friday 5 April 1991.

Mark and Steve Waugh became the first twins to appear in the same Test side when they represented Australia against West Indies at Port of Spain, Trinidad.

They were also the first twins to play together in a Test, adding 58 in an hour and a half for the sixth wicket in Australia's first innings. Mark Waugh top-scored with 64 in the first innings of another rain-affected draw, before taking his first Test wicket, Curtly Ambrose. Torrential rain restricted play to 23 overs on the first day and only eight overs on the second, when the outfield was under water as deep as 8 inches (20 cm) in places.

THE LAST

TEST APPEARANCE BY
VIV RICHARDS

**I.V.A. RICHARDS, WEST INDIES V ENGLAND AT THE OVAL, KENNINGTON,
SURREY, ENGLAND. MONDAY 12 AUGUST 1991.**

West Indies' greatest batsman Viv Richards played his 121st and last Test match in 1991. He was captain as West Indies lost by five wickets to an England side led by Graham Gooch. 'Zap' won the toss and elected to bat, with England making 419 (Robin Smith 109, Gooch 60, Extras 54) before bowling out the tourists for 176 (Phil Tufnell six for 25). Richards, batting unusually low down the order at number eight, scored just two. Gooch enforced the follow-on and the West Indians made 385 (Richie Richardson 121, Richards 60, David 'Syd' Lawrence five for 106). It was not a big enough target and England achieved it with the loss of Gooch, Hugh Morris, Michael Atherton, Robin Smith and Mark Ramprakash. The series ended in a two-all draw. Richards, who had made his Test debut against India in 1974, retired from First Class cricket in 1993. He would have played more Tests had he not signed for Kerry Packer's World Series Cricket. Richards was knighted in 1999. In December 2002 *Wisden Cricketers' Almanack* chose him as the greatest One Day International batsman of all time and the third greatest ever Test batsman.

AIN'T GONNA MAKE ANY DIFFERENCE

Three years earlier Richards had shown an understandable arrogance when West Indies played England under the captaincy of Chris Cowdrey at Headingley, beginning on 21 July 1988. Cowdrey said. 'I was very proud to be appointed England captain... I went out for the tossing of the coin wearing my whites and England blazer. Viv Richards came out wearing a Bob Marley T-shirt, surfing shorts and flip-flops. After tossing the coin, etiquette dictated that I, as England captain, should read our team sheet to the opposing captain. I got no further than four names when Viv said, 'Play who you want, man. Ain't gonna make any difference.' West Indies won by ten wickets.

THE FIRST
TEST MATCH REFEREE
M.J.K. SMITH, AUSTRALIA V INDIA AT BRISBANE CRICKET GROUND, VULTURE STREET, WOOLLOONGABBA, BRISBANE, QUEENSLAND, AUSTRALIA. FRIDAY 29 NOVEMBER 1991.

Former England captain Mike Smith became the first match referee in Tests when he officiated in the first contest between Australia and India in the 1991–1992 season. Australia won by ten wickets.

THE FIRST
BOWLER NO-BALLED FOR BOWLING MORE THAN ONE BOUNCER AT A BATSMAN IN THE SAME OVER
MANOJ PRABHAKAR, INDIA V AUSTRALIA AT BRISBANE CRICKET GROUND, VULTURE STREET, WOOLLOONGABBA, BRISBANE, QUEENSLAND, AUSTRALIA. FRIDAY 29 NOVEMBER 1991.

In a bid to protect batsmen, the Law was changed and bowlers were prevented from bowling more than one bouncer at the same batsman in the same over. The first bowler to fall foul of the new Law was Indian player, Manoj Prabhakar. Five years later, he was booed by Indian fans at Delhi after bowling four overs for 47 against Sri Lanka in the 1995–1996 World Cup. He was dropped from the side and retired. He was then banned because of match-fixing allegations. He stood unsuccessfully for parliament.

THE FIRST
TEST VICTIM OF SHANE WARNE
R.J. SHASTRI, INDIA V AUSTRALIA AT SYDNEY CRICKET GROUND, MOORE PARK, MOORE PARK ROAD, SYDNEY, NEW SOUTH WALES, AUSTRALIA. SUNDAY 5 JANUARY 1992.

Shane Warne did not have a promising start to what became one of the most successful Test careers of all time. He made his Test debut in the third Test of the 1991–1992 rubber between Australia and India. Batting at number ten, he made 20 off 67 balls in 71 minutes, hitting a single four, before he was caught by Chandrakant Pandit off the bowling of Kapil Dev. Australia made 313, including an unbeaten 129 from David Boon. India then batted on the second, third, fourth and fifth days to score 483, with Ravi Shastri making 206 before becoming Warne's first victim, caught by Dean Jones. Warne returned figures of 45-7-150-1. The match ended as a draw.

THE FIRST
WORLD CUP HELD DOWN UNDER
AUSTRALIA AND NEW ZEALAND. SATURDAY 22 FEBRUARY 1992.

The fifth World Cup opened with New Zealand, with a score of 248 for six (Martin Crowe 100 not out, Ken Rutherford 57), beating Australia, who made 211 (David Boon 100, Gavin Larsen three for 30), at Auckland by 37 runs. England, who scored 236 for 9 (Robin Smith 91, Graham Gooch 51), overcame India, who made 227 (Ravi Shastri 57, Dermot Reeve three for 38), at Perth by nine runs. For the first time the teams played in coloured kit with their names on the back and most of the 39 games were played under floodlight, including the Final, when Pakistan beat England by 22 runs. Each game also used two white balls (one at each end so they did not become too dirty).

THIS WAS ALSO: The FIRST time World Cup teams played in coloured kit with their names on their backs

THE FIRST
POST-APARTHEID
SOUTH AFRICA TEST
WEST INDIES V SOUTH AFRICA AT KENSINGTON OVAL, BRIDGETOWN, BARBADOS, WEST INDIES. EASTER SATURDAY 18 APRIL 1992.

South Africa returned to the Test arena in a one-off match against West Indies at Bridgetown, Barbados. Ten of the Springboks made their Test debuts – only captain Kepler Wessels had played before, albeit in Australian colours. After bowling out the home side for 262, the tourists made 345 with a maiden Test century (163) coming from Prince Charles-lookalike Andrew Hudson. He thus became the first South African to make a century on his first international appearance, a feat that was not repeated until Jacques Rudolph scored an undefeated 222 against Bangladesh in April 2003. Wessels made 59 while Jimmy Adams was the most successful West Indian bowler with four for 43. In their second innings the Windies hit 283 (Adams 79, Brian Lara 64) with Allan Donald taking four for 77 and Richard Snell four for 74. Despite 74 from captain Wessels and 52 from Peter Kirsten, the might of Curtley Ambrose (six for 34) and Courtney Walsh (four for 31) saw off the South Africa side for 148. The match was even made into a film, although one review was obviously not written by a cricket fan: 'In a play-by-play look at the final morning, the West Indies team defeats the South African team by an astonishing 52 runs.'

THIS MATCH ALSO INCLUDED: The FIRST South African to make a century on his first international appearance

◆◆◆

THE LAST

TEST APPEARANCE BY
IAN BOTHAM

I.T. Botham, England v Pakistan at Lord's Cricket Ground, St John's Wood Road, St John's Wood, Middlesex, England. Sunday 21 June 1992.

All-rounder legend Ian Botham walked off a Test match pitch for the last time as a player in 1992. Botham had played the first of his 102 Tests against Australia at Trent Bridge in July 1977, when England beat the old enemy by seven wickets. Fourteen years, 10 months and 24 days later, he was on the losing side as Pakistan won the match by two wickets. Botham made a disappointing two and six with the bat and only bowled five overs, comprising three maidens, nought for nine. Botham scored 14 Test centuries and 22 half-centuries. He took 383 wickets with a best of eight for 34. Retiring from cricket completely on 19 July 1993, after playing for Durham against Australia, when he returned the disappointing (by his standards) 11-2-45-0, Botham was knighted in 2007.

THE ONLY
PLAYER BORN IN ONE COUNTRY
WHO PLAYED TEST CRICKET FOR TWO OTHERS

A. J. TRAICOS, SOUTH AFRICA V AUSTRALIA AT KINGSMEAD, DURBAN, KWAZULU-NATAL, SOUTH AFRICA. THURSDAY 5 FEBRUARY 1970; ZIMBABWE V INDIA AT HARARE SPORTS CLUB, HARARE, ZIMBABWE. SUNDAY 18 OCTOBER 1992.

Off-spinner John Traicos made his Test debut for South Africa against Australia at Kingsmead and took three wickets in the game – the second Test of what was the Springboks' last series before international sporting exile. South Africa won by an innings and 129 runs. Traicos also played in the third and fourth Tests before his international career ended for 22 years and 222 days. In October 1992 he was the only member of the first Zimbabwe Test side who had previous experience. He took five for 86. Traicos, who was born at Zagazig, Egypt, fled Zimbabwe for political reasons in 1997 and moved to Perth, Western Australia.

THE ONLY
PLAYER TO SCORE
TEST CENTURIES FOR TWO COUNTRIES

K.C. WESSELS, AUSTRALIA V ENGLAND AT BRISBANE CRICKET GROUND, VULTURE STREET, WOOLLOONGABBA, BRISBANE, QUEENSLAND, AUSTRALIA. SATURDAY 27 NOVEMBER 1982; SOUTH AFRICA V INDIA AT KINGSMEAD, DURBAN, KWAZULU-NATAL, SOUTH AFRICA. FRIDAY 13 NOVEMBER 1992.

Born in South Africa, but unable to play for the Springboks because of international repulsion at its political policy of apartheid, Kepler Wessels played cricket in Australia. He scored a century (162) on his Test debut against England. He made 46 in the second innings as Australia won by 7 wickets. When South Africa were welcomed back into the Test arena Wessels was the natural choice to be the first post-apartheid captain in the Test against West Indies in 1992. His maiden Test century for South Africa came in their second Test, the first in the series against India. He scored 118 in a drawn match.

THE FIRST

BLACK SOUTH AFRICAN
TEST PLAYER

O. Henry, South Africa v India at Kingsmead, Durban, Kwazulu-Natal, South Africa. Friday 13 November 1992.

With the return of South Africa to the Test arena, Omar Henry became the first black player to represent his country. He was also the Springboks' oldest Test debutant at 40 years and 295 days.

THE FIRST

TEST BATSMAN GIVEN OUT
BY THE THIRD UMPIRE

S.R. TENDULKAR, INDIA V SOUTH AFRICA AT KINGSMEAD, DURBAN, KWAZULU-NATAL, SOUTH AFRICA. SATURDAY 14 NOVEMBER 1992.

South Africa's first home Test since March 1970 was full of significant events. It was also the first match in which a third umpire, watching the match on television in the pavilion, was called upon to make decisions. Karl Liebenberg was in front of the television on the second day when Sachin Tendulkar changed his mind about a run and desperately tried to get back to his crease. The square-leg umpire Cyril Mitchley was unsure if Tendulkar had made his ground so he made the shape of a television to Liebenberg who, after 30 seconds, lit a red light to say that Tendulkar was out, for 11. Three umpires stood in the Test, alternating between being in the middle and watching on the television. The match ended in a draw. On 19 June 1993 England batsman Robin Smith became the first player in England, in the Lord's Test against Australia, to be given out thanks to the third umpire Chris Balderstone, watching the match on television. Ian Healey stumped Smith off the bowling of Tim May for 22, as England collapsed to 205 all out and went on to lose the match by an innings and 62 runs.

ROBIN SMITH WAS: The FIRST player in England given out by the third umpire

OUT UNDER LAW 33

On 19 December 2001 Michael Vaughan became the seventh Test batsman to be given out handled the ball. England were on 206 for three at the M. Chinnaswamy Stadium, Bangalore in the third Test against India when off-spinner Sarandeep Singh bowled. Vaughan went to play a sweep shot, missed and the ball became lodged about his person. He used his hand to push it away whereupon the Indian fielders appealed and Vaughan was given out under Law 33. Oddly, if he had picked up the ball and tossed it to a fielder, the Indians almost certainly would not have appealed.

THE FIRST
ENGLAND TEST BATSMAN
GIVEN OUT HANDLED THE BALL
G.A. GOOCH, ENGLAND V AUSTRALIA AT OLD TRAFFORD, MANCHESTER, LANCASHIRE, ENGLAND. MONDAY 7 JUNE 1993.

Playing against Australia at Old Trafford, England captain Graham Gooch became the fifth Test player to be given out handled the ball. The Essex man was on 133 at the time and England lost the match by 179 runs. Gooch said,

'It was an instinctive thing. I couldn't stop myself. If I'd had time to think about it I would have brought my bat up instead. I don't need reminding that we were looking like saving the Test when I got out. Overall we just have to be more competitive.'

THE FIRST
BATSMAN TO SCORE 11,000 TEST RUNS
A.R. BORDER, AUSTRALIA V SOUTH AFRICA AT ADELAIDE OVAL, WAR MEMORIAL DRIVE, NORTH ADELAIDE, SOUTH AUSTRALIA, AUSTRALIA. SATURDAY 29 JANUARY 1994.

On the second day of the third Test against South Africa in the 1993–1994 rubber, Australian captain Allan Border became the first batsman to score

11,000 Test runs when he hit 66. Border went on to score 84 before declaring at 469 for seven. In the second innings he was run out for four, but Australia still won by 191 runs.

—•◦◦◦•—

THE FIRST

TEST MATCH TO REALIZE OVER £2 MILLION AT THE GATE

ENGLAND V WEST INDIES AT LORD'S CRICKET GROUND, ST JOHN'S WOOD ROAD, ST JOHN'S WOOD, MIDDLESEX, ENGLAND. THURSDAY 22 JUNE 1995.

England-West Indies games are only second in popularity to England-Australia Tests, so it was no surprise when the second Test of the 1995 rubber realized gate receipts of more than £2 million. A total of 111,219 fans paid £2,209,321 to watch England win by 72 runs. In total, the five-Test series realized £8,293,637 at the gate.

—•◦◦◦•—

THE LAST

TEST APPEARANCE BY
DICKIE BIRD

H.D. BIRD, ENGLAND V INDIA AT LORD'S CRICKET GROUND, ST JOHN'S WOOD ROAD, ST JOHN'S WOOD, MIDDLESEX, ENGLAND. MONDAY 24 JUNE 1996.

Dickie Bird left the Test arena for the 66th and last time in 1996. His last Test was England v India at Lord's. At the start of the game the two teams formed a guard of honour as he came out and he received a standing ovation from the crowd, whereupon Bird burst into tears. The last player given out by Dickie Bird was Jack Russell, who was lbw to Sourav Ganguly from the Nursery End.

THIS MATCH INCLUDED: The LAST player given out by Dickie Bird

THE ONLY
TEST CRICKETER TO WIN THE DERBY
SHANE WARNE, PAKISTAN. 1996.

In 1996 Shane Warne won the Pakistan Derby. However, this Shane Warne was not the blond Australian spinning legend of cricket but a thoroughbred racehorse.

THE FIRST
MATCH DECIDED ON THE DUCKWORTH/LEWIS METHOD
ZIMBABWE V ENGLAND AT HARARE SPORTS CLUB, HARARE, ZIMBABWE. WEDNESDAY 1 JANUARY 1997.

For years fans, players and statisticians, as well as the game's authorities, have argued over how best to decide matches that cannot be finished in time because of bad weather or other factors. Two British statisticians Frank Duckworth and Tony Lewis created the Duckworth/Lewis (D/L) method to decide outcomes. It is generally accepted to be the best solution, but has caused some controversy.

On 22 March 1992 England played South Africa in a rain-affected World Cup semi final at Sydney, Australia. The match was reduced to 45 overs and England scored 252 for six (Graeme Hick 83) off their allotted span. England had bowled 42.5 overs when it began to rain again and 17 minutes of playing time was lost. When play resumed, the Springboks' target was revised to 252 from 43 overs, leaving a bemused and furious South Africa to get 21 off one ball.

The first match that used the D/L method was the second game of the 1996–1997 Zimbabwe v England One Day International series. England won the toss and put the hosts into bat. Zimbabwe were all out for 200, Andy Flower making 63. The match was interrupted by rain and under the D/L method, England's target was reduced to 185 off 42 overs. When Zimbabwe had bowled 42 overs England had reached 179 for seven, which meant that the hosts won by six runs.

THE FIRST
BATSMAN TO SCORE
TWO UNBEATEN CENTURIES IN A TEST

P.A. DE SILVA, SRI LANKA V PAKISTAN AT SINHALESE SPORTS CLUB GROUND, MAITLAND PLACE, COLOMBO, SRI LANKA. TUESDAY 29 APRIL 1997.

A year after he was named as one of *Wisden*'s five Cricketers of the Year, Sri Lankan Aravinda de Silva became the first man to score two unbeaten centuries in a Test match when he hit 138 and 103 against Pakistan at the Sinhalese Sports Club Ground in Colombo. Despite his achievement, the match ended in a draw.

THE FIRST
FLOODLIT TEST MATCH

AUSTRALIA V NEW ZEALAND AT WESTERN AUSTRALIA CRICKET ASSOCIATION GROUND, NELSON CRESCENT, EAST PERTH, PERTH, WESTERN AUSTRALIA, AUSTRALIA. THURSDAY 20 NOVEMBER 1997.

Floodlights were used for the first time in a Test match as Australia met New Zealand at the WACA, Perth in the second Test of a three-match rubber. The entire third session of the first day's play was conducted under floodlights. Australia won the match by an innings and 70 runs.

THE ONLY
TEST MATCH ABANDONED
BECAUSE OF A DANGEROUS PITCH

WEST INDIES V ENGLAND AT SABINA PARK, KINGSTON, JAMAICA. THURSDAY 29 JANUARY 1998.

The first 1998 Test between West Indies and England at Sabina Park, Kingston, Jamaica became the first Test abandoned because of a poor pitch and dangerous wicket. England won the toss and decided to bat, but after 10.1 overs and 56 minutes they were 17 for three and the players had been hit seven times. The England physiotherapist Wayne Morton spent more time on the pitch than some of the batsmen. The umpires Steve Bucknor and Srinivasaraghavan Venkataraghavan stopped play and, after ten minutes of discussion, the players left the field. Ninety minutes later, the match was abandoned.

THE ONLY
COMMONWEALTH GAMES GOLD MEDALLISTS
**South Africa v Australia at Kelab Aman, Kuala Lumpur, Malaysia.
Saturday 19 September 1998.**

South Africa won the only gold medal for cricket in the Commonwealth Games when they beat Australia by four wickets in Kuala Lumpur. Four years earlier the Ministry of Education in Malaysia had introduced cricket to the school curriculum in the hope of a good showing. However, the semi finals were contested by four giants, South Africa v Sri Lanka and Australia v New Zealand. The Springboks won the toss and elected to field. With three balls of their allotted 50 overs to go, Australia were bowled out for 183, thanks in no small part to captain Steve Waugh, who scored an unbeaten 90. Springbok captain Shaun Pollock took four for 19. South Africa had a target 184 from 50 overs and managed to reach that with four overs to spare. Mike Rindel was the top scorer with 67.

THE LAST
TEST MATCHES ABANDONED WITHOUT A BALL BOWLED
**NEW ZEALAND V INDIA AT CARISBROOK, DUNEDIN, OTAGO, NEW ZEALAND. SUNDAY 20 DECEMBER 1998;
PAKISTAN V ZIMBABWE AT IQBAL STADIUM, FAISALABAD, PAKISTAN. SUNDAY 20 DECEMBER 1998.**

The first Test between New Zealand and India was scheduled for a week before Christmas 1998. No toss was made and there was no play on the first two days, due to heavy rain. On the third day the match was abandoned and the last two days' play cancelled. An unofficial one-day match was scheduled to replace the fourth day. On the same day that the Test was called off, another Test was also abandoned. The third Test had been due to start between Pakistan and Zimbabwe on 17 December 1998, but thick fog had prevented the start of the match. Most of the players did not bother to go to the ground after the second day. The umpires called the match off on the morning of the fourth day. These were the tenth and 11th games in Test history to suffer this fate. The fog gave Zimbabwe their first series win: 1-0.

—◦•◦—

THE ONLY
TIME 100,000 WATCHED
A SINGLE DAY'S PLAY IN A TEST MATCH
INDIA V PAKISTAN AT EDEN GARDENS, CALCUTTA, INDIA. TUESDAY 16 FEBRUARY 1999.

It was estimated that 100,000 people attended the first match of the Asian Test Championship on each of the first four days. Around 465,000 people watched the game, which Pakistan won by 46 runs.

—◦•◦—

THE ONLY
TEST CAPTAIN TO
TAKE TWO HAT-TRICKS
WASIM AKRAM, PAKISTAN V SRI LANKA AT GADDAFI STADIUM, LAHORE, PAKISTAN. SATURDAY 6 MARCH 1999.

In the Asian Test Championship of 1998–1999 Pakistan captain Wasim Akram became the only Test captain to take a hat-trick when he captured the wickets of Sri Lanka's Kaluwitharana, Bandaratilleke and Wickramasinghe in their first innings. The match ended in a draw and Wasim Akram did not even get the Man of the Match honour. Eight days late, the two teams met again and Wasim Akram took another hat-trick, taking the wickets of Gunawardene, Vaas and Jayawardene in the second innings, to become the only bowler to take two Test hat-tricks as captain.

THE ONLY
INNINGS FORFEITED IN A
TEST MATCH

South Africa v England, Supersport Park, Centurion, Gauteng, South Africa. Tuesday 18 January 2000.

When England toured South Africa in 1999–2000 they lost two of the first four Test matches, giving the rubber to the Springboks. On the first day of play (14 January 2000) of the fifth and final Test South Africa scored 155 for six, before rain prevented play on the next three days. South African captain Hansie Cronje proposed to England captain Nasser Hussain that his team bat until they reached 250 at which time they would declare, and both sides would forfeit an innings, leaving England 251 to win. Hussain agreed and in the end the Springboks made 248. At the time the Laws allowed only one side to forfeit an innings so England were recorded as nought for nought declared. England eventually made 251 for eight and won by two wickets. It was later revealed that the Cronje had been asked by a bookie to ensure the match did not end without a positive result.

THE ONLY
TEST MATCH IN WHICH A PART
OF ALL FOUR INNINGS OCCURRED ON SAME DAY

ENGLAND V WEST INDIES AT LORD'S CRICKET GROUND, ST JOHN'S WOOD ROAD, ST JOHN'S WOOD, MIDDLESEX, ENGLAND. FRIDAY 30 JUNE 2000.

On 1 July 2000 England beat West Indies by two wickets in the second Test at Lord's. England won the toss and decided to field. The match became a wicketfest with one falling every 22 deliveries and on the second day a part of all four innings occurred – the only such incident in Test history. The day began with the West Indies first innings at 267 for nine. West Indies then bowled England out for 134 before the home side dismissed the tourists for just 54. At close of play England, in their second innings, were nought for no loss. England made their target, reaching 191 for the loss of eight wickets.

THE FIRST

PLAYER SUSPENDED FOR BALL TAMPERING

Waqar Younis, Pakistan v Sri Lanka at Paikiasothy Saravanamuttu Stadium, Colombo, Sri Lanka. Sunday 9 July 2000.

In 2000 Pakistan's Waqar Younis became the first player in First Class cricket suspended for ball tampering. He was banned for playing in one match after he was found guilty of tampering with the ball during the one-day game in Sri Lanka on 8 July 2000 at Colombo. Tournament referee John Reid also fined Waqar half of his match fee for lifting the seam off the ball. Pakistani captain Moin Khan and all-rounder Azhar Mahmood were also punished for their involvement. Waqar and Mahmood were seen on television altering the ball. Mahmood was fined 30 per cent of his fee and Moin was severely reprimanded for 'allowing the spirit of the game to be impaired'. Waqar's punishment was more severe than Mahmood's because Reid had warned him for a similar offence during the third Test against Sri Lanka at Kandy the previous week. None of the players appealed the penalty.

THE FIRST

BANGLADESHI TEST CAPTAIN

Naimur Rahman, Bangladesh v India at Bangabandhu National Stadium, Dhaka, Bangladesh. Friday 10 November 2000.

With the granting of Test status on 26 June 2000, Bangladesh became the tenth country to play Test matches. Their first Test was against India and their first captain was Naimur Rahman, a right arm off-spinner. He was also known as Durjoy, which means 'Invincible', an unusual nickname for a man who stands a smidgeon over 5 feet (1.52 m) tall. Bangladesh won the toss and went into bat, making a highly creditable 400 with Aminul Islam scoring 145, thus becoming the first Bangladeshi to score a Test century. Sunil Joshi took five for 142. India responded with 429 and Rahman took six for 132, including the wickets of Sachin Tendulkar and

Sourav Ganguly. Disastrously, in their second innings Bangladesh collapsed to 91 all out and India easily attained their target of 63, finishing on 64 for one in a minute over an hour of play. Rahman played eight Tests before he suffered a loss of form and consequently his job and place in the team.

THIS MATCH INCLUDED: The FIRST Bangladeshi to score a Test century

━●◆●━

THE ONLY
STADIUM TO HAVE HOSTED
AN INAUGURAL HOME FIXTURE
FOR TWO TEST NATIONS
BANGABANDHU NATIONAL STADIUM, DHAKA, BANGLADESH. FRIDAY 10 NOVEMBER 2000.

The last Test match held in the only stadium to have hosted an inaugural home fixture for two Test nations ended in a draw between Bangladesh and Zimbabwe on 18 January 2005. On 1 January 1955, as the Dacca Stadium when Dacca was the capital of East Pakistan, it hosted the inaugural Test match for Pakistan (against India which finished in a draw). On 10 November 2000 India were again the guests, as Bangladesh became the tenth nation to attain Test status, and the venue was now called the Bangabandhu National Stadium, Dhaka. From 1 March 2005 the stadium has been used exclusively for the Bangladeshi national football team.

━●◆●━

THE FIRST
TEST IN WHICH ALL 11
FIELDERS APPEARED ON THE SCORECARD
South Africa v West Indies at Sabina Park, Kingston, Jamaica. Sunday 22 April 2001.

South Africa dismissed West Indies in their second innings for 301 in the fifth Test in 2001. It was the first time in Test history in which all 11 players on the fielding side featured on the scorecard. It didn't help much – West Indies won by 130 runs. No one scored a century and only Shaun Pollock managed to take five wickets in an innings.

THE FIRST

BOWLER RECORDED AT MORE THAN 100 MPH (161 KPH)

SHOAIB AKHTAR, PAKISTAN V NEW ZEALAND AT GADAFFI STADIUM, LAHORE, PAKISTAN. SATURDAY 27 APRIL 2002.

It is more than likely that a number of bowlers have delivered balls at more than 100 mph (161 kph) but in the spring of 2001 Shoaib Akhtar of Pakistan became the first man to be recorded doing so when his delivery hit 100.04 mph during a One Day International against New Zealand in Lahore. Craig McMillan was the batsman facing him down. The record was not recognized by the ICC because it could not agree on a method of measuring speeds.

THE ONLY

TEAM TO SCORE FEWER THAN 40 RUNS IN A WORLD CUP INNINGS

CANADA V SRI LANKA AT BOLAND BANK PARK, PAARL, WESTERN CAPE, SOUTH AFRICA. WEDNESDAY 19 FEBRUARY 2003.

Admittedly it is one of the ICC cricketing minnows, but Canada were probably expecting a better score than 36 against Sri Lanka, not so long ago a minor team themselves. Five players made a duck (one was nought not out) and none reached double figures. It took Sri Lanka just 4.4 overs and 18 minutes to achieve a nine-wicket victory.

THE ONLY
BATSMAN TO SCORE 400
IN TEST CRICKET

B.C. LARA, WEST INDIES V ENGLAND AT ANTIGUA RECREATION GROUND, ST JOHN'S, ANTIGUA. MONDAY 12 APRIL 2004.

West Indies captain Brian Lara became the only player to score a quadruple century in Test cricket when he completed his mammoth innings of 400 not out in the fourth Test against England. He regained the record for the highest individual Test innings that he had lost to Matthew Hayden earlier in the season. The West Indians declared on 751 for five as the Trinidadian left-hander faced 582 deliveries, hitting 43 fours and four sixes, reaching the milestone just over two hours into the third day at Antigua Recreation Ground, St John's, Antigua. He survived an opportunity on 359 when Papua New Guinea-born debutant wicketkeeper Geraint Jones dropped what appeared to be a nick down the leg side. England were bowled out for 285 and the home side enforced the follow-on, but a century from captain Michael Vaughan (140) ensured the match fizzled out into a draw.

THE FIRST
TEST WIN BY
BANGLADESH

BANGLADESH V ZIMBABWE, AT M.A. AZIZ STADIUM, CHITTAGONG, BANGLADESH. MONDAY 10 JANUARY 2005.

Bangladesh won their first Test match – at the 35th attempt, when they beat a weakened Zimbabwe at Chittagong, by 226 runs. Their record prior to the match was 31 defeats and three draws. Bangladesh won the toss and decided to bat. They made 488 – their highest Test score – but, oddly, the innings contained no centurions (top scorer was their captain Habibul Bashar on 94). Their innings did, however, include four half-centuries, a 48 and a 49. Zimbabwe were bowled out for 312 with Mohammad Rafique taking five for 65. Captain-wicketkeeper Tatenda Taibu was the top scorer on 92. Bangladesh made 204 for nine when they declared their second innings and bowled Zimbabwe out for 154, with Enamul Haque taking six for 45. The second Test in the rubber ended in a draw, which meant that Bangladesh had also won their first Test series.

The country celebrated wildly and in the outlying village of Khulna one Bangladeshi celebrated the victory by firing his gun into the air. As he did so, he managed to shoot himself in the shoulder, causing him to drop the rifle which let off another round as it hit the earth. The bullet hit the front wheel of an approaching police car that had been summoned to the area to bring calm to the streets.

THE FIRST
UMPIRE TO STAND IN
100 TESTS

S.A. BUCKNOR, INDIA V PAKISTAN AT EDEN GARDENS, CALCUTTA, INDIA. WEDNESDAY 16 MARCH 2005.

Born at Montego Bay, Jamaica on 31 May 1946, Steve Bucknor refereed football matches before standing in his first international (a One Day International between West Indies and India at Antigua on 18 March 1989). A month later, on 28 April, he officiated in his first Test, also between West Indies and India at Sabina Park, Kingston, Jamaica. He stood in the World Cups in 1992, 1996, 1999, 2003 and 2007. Bucknor became the first umpire to officiate in 100 Tests when he stood in the match between India and Pakistan at Eden Gardens, Calcutta. On 23 February 2009 Bucknor announced his retirement after standing in more than 125 Tests. His final Test was the third match between South Africa and Australia at Cape Town, beginning on 19 March 2009.

THE FIRST

IDENTICAL TWINS
TO PLAY IN THE SAME TEST SIDE

J.A.H. MARSHALL AND H.J.H. MARSHALL, NEW ZEALAND V AUSTRALIA
AT EDEN PARK, AUCKLAND, NEW ZEALAND. SATURDAY 26 MARCH 2005.

James and Hamish Marshall became the first identical twins to play Test
cricket in the same side when they appeared for New Zealand against
Australia. Australia won the match by nine wickets. James, making his
Test debut, opened the batting for the Kiwis and made 29. His twin went
in at number three and scored 76. In the second innings they made three and
seven respectively.

THE FIRST

INTERNATIONAL
TWENTY20 MATCH IN
ENGLAND

ENGLAND V AUSTRALIA AT ROSE BOWL, BOTLEY ROAD, SOUTHAMPTON, HAMPSHIRE, ENGLAND.
MONDAY 13 JUNE 2005.

England (179 for eight) beat Australia (79) by 100 runs in the first Twenty20
international in England, played at the Rose Bowl, Hampshire. For a score
of 34 and three catches Kevin Pietersen was made Man of the Match.

THE LAST

TELEVISION BROADCAST IN
ENGLAND BY RICHIE BENAUD

ENGLAND V AUSTRALIA AT THE OVAL, KENNINGTON, SURREY, ENGLAND.
MONDAY 12 SEPTEMBER 2005.

After a phenomenally successful career as a cricketer, Richie Benaud
began a phenomenally successful career as a broadcaster, primarily for the
BBC in England (beginning on the wireless in 1960) and for Nine Network

in Australia. He played in or commentated on around 500 Test matches. His last broadcast in England was near the end of the final day of the fifth Test at The Oval in 2005. His last words were '[Glenn] McGrath got his man [Kevin Pietersen], and up in the commentary box now, Mark Nicholas and Tony Greig.'

THE FIRST
INTERNATIONAL TWENTY20 MATCH IN
AUSTRALIA

AUSTRALIA V SOUTH AFRICA AT BRISBANE CRICKET GROUND, VULTURE STREET, WOOLLOONGABBA, BRISBANE, QUEENSLAND, AUSTRALIA. MONDAY 9 JANUARY 2006.

Australia (209 for three) beat South Africa (114 all out) in the first international Twenty20 game to be held in Australia, before a crowd of 38,894 people at the Gabba, Brisbane. Oddly, rather than their names, the players' shirts bore their nicknames.

THE ONLY
BOWLER TO TAKE A HAT-TRICK IN
THE FIRST OVER OF A TEST MATCH

I. PATHAN, INDIA V PAKISTAN AT NATIONAL STADIUM, KARACHI, PAKISTAN. SUNDAY 29 JANUARY 2006.

Three years after his Test debut, Irfan Pathan opened the bowling for India in the third Test of the 2005–2006 rubber and, after delivering three balls, had Salman Butt caught by Indian captain Rahul Dravid. With his next ball Pathan had Pakistan captain Younis Khan out lbw and completed his hat-trick by bowling Mohammad Yousuf. Six balls and Pakistan were nought for three. Pathan took five for 61 as the home side recovered to make 245, thanks to a century from wicketkeeper Kamran Akmal. Batting at number eight, Pathan scored 40, including six fours and one six. His second innings figures were not so good, taking just one for 106 and making just four with the bat as Pakistan won by 341 runs. Pathan was also the first Indian to take a hat-trick in an away Test.

THIS MATCH ALSO INCLUDED: The FIRST Indian to take a hat-trick in an away Test

THE FIRST
SIKH TO PLAY TEST CRICKET
FOR ENGLAND

M.S. PANESAR, ENGLAND V INDIA AT VIDARBHA CRICKET ASSOCIATION GROUND, NAGPUR, INDIA. WEDNESDAY 1 MARCH 2006.

Luton-born Mudhsuden Singh 'Monty' Panesar made his First Class debut for Northamptonshire in 2001. Five years later, he appeared at Nagpur in the first Test of the 2005–2006 rubber, becoming the first Sikh to represent any country other than India. Panesar made nine with the bat and took two for 73 and one for 58. His first Test victim was Sachin Tendulkar whom he had lbw for 16. He bowled Mohammad Kaif when he was nine short of his ton and Panesar's second innings victim was Rahul Dravid, bowled for 71. The match was played without a rest day and ended on 5 March 2006 in a draw.

THE FIRST
AFGHANISTAN
INTERNATIONAL

AFGHANISTAN V MCC AT BRABOURNE STADIUM, MUMBAI, INDIA. THURSDAY 23 MARCH 2006.

Afghanistan played their first international match against MCC at Brabourne Stadium, Mumbai. In their 45 overs the Afghans scored 361 for seven, including an unbeaten 116 in 44 balls, which included 13 sixes, from Mohammed Nabi. MCC were dismissed for 171 and captain Mike Gatting was out for a duck.

THE FIRST

IRELAND ONE DAY INTERNATIONAL

IRELAND V ENGLAND AT CIVIL SERVICE NORTH OF IRELAND CRICKET CLUB, STORMONT ESTATE, UPPER NEWTOWNARDS ROAD, BELFAST, NORTHERN IRELAND. TUESDAY 13 JUNE 2006.

Ireland played their first official One Day International in 2006. Their opponents were England at Stormont, Belfast. Obviously all the Ireland team made their international debuts that day but England also had three debutants – Glen Chapple (his only international appearance, he scored 14 and took nought for 14), Jamie Dalrymple and Ed Joyce. The oddest thing about Ed Joyce's debut that day was that his brother Dominick was also making his debut, but playing for Ireland.

THE FIRST

BLACK CAPTAIN OF THE SOUTH AFRICA TEST SIDE

A.G. PRINCE, SOUTH AFRICA V SRI LANKA AT SINHALESE SPORTS CLUB GROUND, COLOMBO, SRI LANKA. THURSDAY 27 JULY 2006.

Ashwell Prince became the first black captain of the South Africa Test side when he led the team in the first match against Sri Lanka, following the unavailability of Graeme Smith and Jacques Kallis. Prince won the toss and elected to bat, but the Sri Lankans dumped the Springboks out for 169 with Prince contributing just a single run. Sri Lanka began unimpressively and were 14 for two until captain Mahela Jayawardene and Kumar Sangakkara came to the wicket. They shared a world record partnership of 624 before the third wicket fell. Jayawardene scored 374 and Sangakkara was not far behind on 287. South Africa responded with a respectable 434, but not one player reached triple figures and Sri Lanka won by an innings and 153 runs. In the One Day International series that followed Prince lost the captaincy to Mark Boucher.

THE ONLY

CAPTAIN TO FORFEIT A TEST MATCH

INZAMAM UL-HAQ, PAKISTAN V ENGLAND AT THE OVAL, KENNINGTON, SURREY, ENGLAND. SUNDAY 20 AUGUST 2006.

After umpires Darrell Hair and Billy Doctrove accused them of ball-tampering, Pakistan, led by captain Inzamam ul-Haq, refused to retake the field in the Oval Test. The umpires awarded England five penalty runs and the choice of a replacement ball, after ruling that Pakistan had illegally altered the ball. When the Pakistanis stayed in their dressing room, the umpires declared that the match could not be finished and left the field with the England team. The Pakistanis eventually returned, to find an empty arena. Inzamam became the first captain in history to forfeit a Test match and was later charged with bringing the game into disrepute. On 28 September 2006 the allegations of ball-tampering were dismissed, but he was found guilty and suspended for four One Day Internationals. The ICC later changed the result and declared the match a draw.

THE ONLY

TEAM TO SCORE 400 IN A WORLD CUP MATCH

INDIA V BERMUDA AT QUEEN'S PARK OVAL, PORT OF SPAIN, TRINIDAD. MONDAY 19 MARCH 2007.

Having surprisingly lost their first World Cup match to Bangladesh, India were out to show the world that they could play cricket. India made 413 for seven after Bermuda won the toss, went against W.G. Grace's maxim and decided to field. The decision seemed justified when they took the first Indian wicket (Robin Uthappa) when the score was on three. However, the next wicket did not fall until the score reached 205. Virender Sehwag (who was to win the Man of the Match award) hit 118 as India took the Bermudan bowling apart. They became the only team to score more than 400 by the time their innings ended after 50 overs. Bermudan opener Oliver Pitcher lasted just six balls before being out for a duck and, although it took India 43.1 overs to get rid of the Bermudans, they never looked like reaching the target and were all out for 156 (Extras was the second highest scorer), making India the winners by 257 runs.

THE FIRST

ENGLAND WICKETKEEPER
TO SCORE A HUNDRED
ON TEST DEBUT

M.J. PRIOR, ENGLAND V WEST INDIES AT LORD'S CRICKET GROUND, ST JOHN'S WOOD ROAD, ST JOHN'S WOOD, MIDDLESEX, ENGLAND. FRIDAY 18 MAY 2007.

Matt Prior represented England at all ages, up to, and including being part of the Under-19 squad, making his Sussex debut in 2001. He became the first England wicketkeeper to score a century on his first appearance in Test cricket when he hit an unbeaten 126 against West Indies at Lord's in the first match of the rubber. Prior's was one of four centuries in England's 553 for five declared. Prior's hundred came off 105 balls in 114 minutes and included 16 fours. Prior was also one of three South African-born players representing England in the Test and one of four foreign-born players in the side (Andrew Strauss, Owais Shah and Kevin Pietersen being the others). He followed his ton with 75 at Headingley.

THE ONLY
BATSMAN TO SCORE
100 SIXES
IN TEST MATCHES
A. GILCHRIST, AUSTRALIA V SRI LANKA AT BELLERIVE OVAL, BELLERIVE, HOBART, TASMANIA, AUSTRALIA. SATURDAY 17 NOVEMBER 2007.

Adam Gilchrist holds the world records for the most dismissals by a wicketkeeper in One Day Internationals (417 caught and 55 stumped) and by an Australian wicketkeeper in Tests (397 caught and 37 stumped). He is also the only player to score 50 or more in three consecutive World Cup Finals (1999, 2003 and 2007). Between 1999 and 2008 Gilchrist played 96 Tests for Australia, scoring 5,570 runs with a top score of 204 not out and an average of 47.60. In those Tests he hit 677 fours and exactly 100 sixes. His 100th six came in the second Test between Australia and Sri Lanka at Hobart. It was Gilchrist's 92nd Test and he scored an unbeaten 67 as Australia won by 96 runs.

ADAM GILCHRIST IS ALSO: The ONLY player to score 50 or more in three consecutive World Cup Finals

THE FIRST
PINK BALL
MCC V SCOTLAND AT LORD'S CRICKET GROUND, ST JOHN'S WOOD ROAD, ST JOHN'S WOOD, MIDDLESEX, ENGLAND. TUESDAY 22 APRIL 2008.

With the advent of one day cricket the authorities began experimenting with different coloured balls. Orange and yellow did not pass muster with the tests required and were not suitable for First Class cricket because they wear differently. White balls have been used since 1979, although some players claim that a white ball swings more than a red ball during the first half of an innings and also wears more quickly. The first match in which a pink ball was used took place between MCC and Scotland. The first findings seemed to indicate that a pink ball was visible for longer than a white ball. It remains to be seen if Tests will be played with pink balls.

THE LAST
PLAYER TO APPEAR IN
INTERNATIONAL
CRICKET WITHOUT PLAYING A FIRST CLASS MATCH

D.A. Warner, Australia v South Africa at Melbourne Cricket Ground, Jolimont, Melbourne, Victoria, Australia. Sunday 11 January 2009.

Left-handed opening batsman David Warner, 22 years old, was selected for the first Twenty20 international against South Africa of the 2008–2009 season, despite having never previously played First Class cricket. It was the first time such a selection had been made since the first Test in 1877. Warne repaid the faith by scoring 89 off 43 balls, including seven fours and six sixes. Warner scored what was then the second fastest 50 in Twenty20 internationals. It was also the second highest score on a Twenty20 international debut. A year later, on 23 February 2010, Warner hit 67 off 29 balls with his 50 coming up in just 18 balls, beating his previous best of 19 deliveries. Warner's First Class debut came at the Sydney Cricket Ground on 5 March 2009 in the last match of the 2008–2009 Sheffield Shield between New South Wales and Western Australia.

THE ONLY
PLAYER TO SCORE ODI CENTURIES
FOR TWO COUNTRIES

E.J.G. MORGAN, IRELAND V CANADA AT JAFFERY SPORTS CLUB GROUND, NAIROBI, KENYA. SUNDAY 4 FEBRUARY 2007; BANGLADESH V ENGLAND AT SHERE BANGLA NATIONAL STADIUM, MIRPUR, DHAKA, BANGLADESH. TUESDAY 2 MARCH 2010.

In the ICC World Cricket League Division One Dublin-born Eoin Morgan scored 115 of Ireland's 308 for seven from their 50 overs. Despite his efforts, Canada won the match by six wickets with two balls remaining. It was also Morgan's first century in a One Day International, having been run out for 99 on his debut against Scotland. Deciding that he would have a better career and future with England, Morgan switched his allegiance in 2009. In the second ODI against Bangladesh Morgan scored an unbeaten 110.

THE ONLY
TEST MATCH ABANDONED
BECAUSE OF TERRORISM
PAKISTAN V SRI LANKA AT GADDAFI STADIUM, LAHORE, PAKISTAN. TUESDAY 3 MARCH 2009.

The Sri Lanka Test team bus was attacked by a dozen terrorists near Liberty Market as it drove to the Gaddafi Stadium in Lahore on the third day of the second Test against Pakistan. Sri Lanka captain Mahela Jayawardene, vice-captain Kumar Sangakkara and five other players, Ajantha Mendis, Thilan Samaraweera, Tharanga Paranavitana, Suranga Lakmal and Chaminda Vaas, plus the assistant coach Paul Farbrace, received minor injuries, but six policemen and a civilian driver were murdered in the assault.

'The bus came under attack as we were driving to the stadium, the gunmen targeted the wheels of the bus first and then the bus,' Jayawardene said. 'We all dived to the floor to take cover.' Sangakkara said, 'Thilan has a shrapnel wound in his leg, but he is fine. Paranavitana had shrapnel in his chest, but thank God it wasn't very deep and just on the surface. I had shrapnel injuries in my shoulder, but they have all been removed and I'm okay now. Ajantha had shrapnel in his neck and scalp, but he, too, has had medical attention and is fine. Everyone else is perfectly all right.' The reserve umpire Ahsan Raza was also injured in the attack.

The Sri Lanka team was evacuated from Gaddafi Stadium and the Test abandoned. Ironically, the Sri Lankans were playing in Pakistan because India had refused to let its Test side into the country, following the terror attack in Mumbai in November 2008. The Test series was the first played in Pakistan since October 2007. Former Pakistan Test captain Imran Khan said, 'This was one of the worst security failures in Pakistan. The Pakistan government guaranteed the Sri Lankan cricket team that they would provide them security. The security provided was shameful.'

On the first two days of the Test Sri Lanka had made 606 with Samaraweera making 214 before being run out. Tillakaratne Dilshan made 145 before he, too, was run out and Sangakkara made 104. Umar Gul was Pakistan's most successful bowler, taking six for 135. In reply Pakistan had made 100 for one before the match was abandoned.

FINHAM LIBRARY

BIBLIOGRAPHY

Books

Allen, David Rayvern *The Guinness Book of Cricket Extras* (Enfield: Guinness Superlatives, 1988)

Bailey, Philip, Philip Thorn and Peter Wynne-Thomas *Who's Who of Cricketers* (London: Newnes, 1984)

Batty, Clive *The Ashes Miscellany* (London: VSP, 2006)

Beadle, Jeremy *Jeremy Beadle's Today's The Day* (London: W.H. Allen, 1979)

Dawson, Marc *The Bumper Book of Cricket Useless Information* (London: Metro, 2009)

Fingleton, J. H. *The Immortal Victor Trumper* (London: Collins, 1978)

Frindall, Bill *The Guinness Book of Cricket Facts and Feats* (Enfield: Guinness Superlatives, 1983)

The Wisden Book of Test Cricket Volume 1 1877–1977 (3rd ed) (London: Queen Anne Press, 1990)

The Wisden Book of Test Cricket Volume II 1977–1989 (3rd ed) (London: Queen Anne Press, 1990)

NatWest Playfair World Cup 1999 (London: Headline, 1999)

Ask Bearders (London: BBC Books, 2009)

Green, Benny *Wisden Anthology 1864–1900* (London: Macdonald & Jane's, 1979)

Wisden Anthology 1900–1940 (London: Queen Anne Press, 1980)

Wisden Anthology 1940–1963 (London: Queen Anne Press, 1982)

Wisden Anthology 1963–1982 (London: Queen Anne Press, 1983)

The Wisden Book of Cricketers' Lives (London: Queen Anne Press, 1986)

Haigh, Gideon *Peter The Lord's Cat and Other Unexpected Obituaries From Wisden* (London: Aurum, 2006)

Halliday, Stephen *London Underground Facts* (Newton Abbot: David & Charles, 2009)

Hansard, 13 November 1990, Column 464

Harris, Cyril M. *What's in a Name?* (Harrow: Capital History, 2005)

Hayes, Dean *Cricket Oddities* (Stroud: Stadia, 2008)

L'Estrange, Jonathan *The Big Book of More Sports Insults* (London: Weidenfeld & Nicolson, 2005)

Long, David *The Little Book of The London Underground* (Stroud: The History Press, 2009)

Lynch, Steven *Wisden on The Ashes* (London: John Wisden, 2009)

Major, Sir John *More Than a Game* (London: HarperPerennial, 2008)

Martin-Jenkins, Christopher *The Complete Who's Who of Test Cricketers* (London: Orbis, 1980)

Matthew, H.C.G. and Sir Brian Harrison (eds) *Oxford Dictionary of National Biography* (Oxford: Oxford University Press, 2004)

McWhirter, Norris (ed) *The Guinness Book of Records 1984* (Enfield: Guinness Superlatives, 1983)

Montague, Trevor *A to Z of Britain and Ireland* (London: Sphere, 2009)

Moss, Stephen *Wisden Anthology 1978-2006* (Alton: John Wisden, 2006)

Motson, John *Motson's FA Cup Odyssey* (London: Robson Books, 2005)

Playfair Cricket Annual, various editions

Robertson, Patrick *The New Shell Book of Firsts* (London: Headline, 1994)

Rundell, Michael *The Wisden Dictionary of Cricket* (London: A&C Black, 2006)

Scott, Les *Bats, Balls & Bails: The Essential Cricket Book* (London: Bantam Press, 2009)

Seddon, Peter *Pickles The World Cup Dog and Other Unusual Football Obituaries* (London: Aurum, 2007)

Tibballs, Geoff *Cricket's Greatest Characters* (London: JR Books, 2008)

Wallechinsky, David *The Complete Book of the Olympics* (London: Aurum Press, 2004)

Ward, Andrew *Cricket's Strangest Matches* (London: Robson Books, 2002)

White, John *The England Cricket Miscellany* (London: Carlton Books, 2006)

Wickham Legg, L.G. (ed) *The Dictionary of National Biography 1931–1940* (London: Oxford University Press, 1949)

Wisden Cricketers' Almanack, various editions

Woolgar, Jason *England's Test Cricketers 1877–1996* (London: Robert Hale, 1997)

Wright, Graeme *A Wisden Collection* (London: Bloomsbury, 2004)

Wynne-Thomas, Peter *The Hamlyn A–Z of Cricket Records* (Feltham: Hamlyn, 1983)

Magazines

The Cricketer, The Cricketer Quarterly International, Wisden Cricket Monthly, The Wisden Cricketer

Newspapers

The Daily Telegraph, The Times

Websites

Video sites have been especially useful as they have enabled me to view footage of some stories and, where necessary, correct previous accounts.

━━◆━◆━◆━━

ACKNOWLEDGEMENTS

Executive Editor - Trevor Davies
Managing Editor - Clare Churly
Creative Director - Tracy Killick
Designer - Geoff Fennell
Production Manager - David Hearn